**THE
SOCIAL
GRACES**
Incorporated
7 1 3 9
Woodley
A v e n u e
Van Nuys, CA
9 1 4 0 6

6/25/10
TO: TAD

Enjoy

Thanks
Brad

CIRQUE DU SOLEIL

20 YEARS UNDER THE SUN

CIRQUE DU SOLEIL

20 YEARS UNDER THE SUN

AN AUTHORIZED HISTORY

Written by Tony Babinski

Art Direction by Kristian Manchester

CIRQUE DU SOLEIL

HARRY N. ABRAMS, INC., PUBLISHERS

Editor: Christopher Sweet
Editorial Assistant: Sigi Nacson
Production Manager: Jane Searle

Library of Congress Cataloging-in-Publication Data

Babinski, Tony.
Cirque du Soleil: 20 Years Under the Sun / text by Tony
Babinski; art direction by Kristian Manchester.
And design by Christian Bélanger, Kristian Manchester,
Kevin Massé, Nicolas Saint-Cyr, Norman Terrault.
p. cm.
Includes bibliographical references and index.

ISBN 0-8109-4636-X (hardcover)
1. Cirque du Soleil--History.
2. Circus--Quebec (Province)--History.
I. Title: Cirque du Soleil: 20 Years Under the Sun.
II. Title: 20 Years Under the Sun. III. Title.

GV1821.C578B33 2004
791.3'09--dc22
2003026669

Printed and bound in China

10 9 8 7 6 5 4 3 2 1

 Harry N. Abrams, Inc.
100 Fifth Avenue
New York, N.Y. 10011
www.abramsbooks.com

Abrams is a subsidiary of

➤ WELCOME TO A CELEBRATION, IN WORDS AND PICTURES, OF TWENTY YEARS OF CIRQUE DU SOLEIL.

What you hold in your hands is a chronological history of Cirque du Soleil, from its earliest days to the beginning of 2004. You'll read about our origins, our struggles and victories, and our productions through the years.

So many talented, dedicated people have been part of the Cirque du Soleil story:
• The pioneers who were there in the early years, putting their hearts and soul on the line without any guarantee of making it to the big time.
• The creators and artists, whose incredible work on and off the stage is vital to our company.
• The thousands of employees who keep us going, day in and day out, in Montreal, Las Vegas, Orlando, Amsterdam, Melbourne, and on tour around the world.
• And the many friends, collaborators, and partners who have supported us on the journey.

Many of them have been there with us for years, and a special few have been there from the very beginning. They all have wonderful stories to tell that reflect their passion and commitment. I offer them my heartfelt thanks.

So much of what Cirque has done is still onstage, on-screen, or in the air, waiting to be discovered by audiences new and old. We've tried to capture that magic on the printed page.

None of it would have happened without you, the audience. If we've made it this far, it's only been because of your support and approval, for which we are deeply thankful. In that spirit of gratitude, we dedicate this book to you.

Let the celebration begin!

Guy Laliberté, Founder and Guide
Montreal, 2004

♥

TABLE OF CONTENTS

PART 1: THE SUN RISES: EARLY YEARS

PART 2: CREATING WORLDS UPON WORLDS

PART 3: STILL SHINING: 2000 — PRESENT DAY

PART 1

THE SUN RISES

EARLY YEARS

CIRQUE DU SOLEIL'S FIRST OFFICIAL PERFORMANCE TOOK PLACE
ON JUNE 16, 1984, IN A SMALL QUEBEC TOWN CALLED GASPÉ.
GUY LALIBERTÉ, ITS FOUNDER, HAD CREATED CIRQUE WITH A SIMPLE
PLAN. CIRQUE DU SOLEIL WOULD BE QUEBEC'S FIRST-EVER
HOMEGROWN CIRCUS, AND IT WOULD PROVIDE LALIBERTÉ AND
HIS FRIENDS WITH A WAY TO TRAVEL, HAVE FUN, AND MAKE
AUDIENCES HAPPY. TWENTY YEARS LATER, THAT SIMPLE PLAN HAS
TURNED INTO AN INTERNATIONAL ENTERTAINMENT SUCCESS STORY.
HOW DID IT HAPPEN? AND WHY? THE ANSWER BEGINS IN DREAMS.
CIRQUE DU SOLEIL WAS BORN OF THE WILD ASPIRATIONS OF A
HANDFUL OF INDIVIDUALS HUNGRY FOR LIGHT, FREEDOM,
AND THE GIFTS OF THE IMAGINATION.

THE DREAMING LAND

QUEBEC ROOTS

CHAPTER

1

> **CIRQUE DU SOLEIL COULD ONLY HAVE BEEN BORN IN QUEBEC. THOUGH CIRQUE NOW BELONGS TO THE WORLD, QUEBEC SHAPED CIRQUE DU SOLEIL AND NURTURED IT IN ITS EARLY YEARS.**

THE DREAMING LAND

Quebec also gave Cirque du Soleil's creators a worldview unique in North America. With roots in Europe stretching back to 1534, Quebec has always had one foot in the Old World, and one in the New. As a francophone culture dwarfed by its neighbors, Quebec has often been on the outside, looking in.

Until the middle of the twentieth century, much of Quebec was French-speaking, rural, Roman Catholic, and isolated.

Dominique Lemieux, one of the costume designers who helped give Cirque du Soleil its distinct visual identity, believes that Quebec's isolation gave its artists a singular, imaginative take on the world. "Quebecois people are close to the earth," she explains. "That made us inventive and turned us into storytellers." As the century wore on, the Quebecois imagination, nurtured by solitude, grew hand-in-hand with a hunger for the outside world.

02/

STARVING FOR CONNECTION

René Dupéré, one of the composers who shaped Cirque du Soleil's signature sound, grew up in a town of just 5,000. Like so many who built Cirque with him, he was eagerly interested in the larger world.

"I was raised with an open spirit," he says. "My father would make me read this series of books called Countries and Peoples, about all the countries in the world. There were photos of places and people who were different from us in our village. I was so taken with them."

Beginning in high school, Dupéré became especially interested in music from other parts of the world. "I had two priests teaching me who were crazy about not only classical music but ethnic music as well," he remembers. "They would have us listen to music from Yugoslavia, from Greece, from the Balkans. That was a real turning point in my life." The effect can still be heard in Dupéré's music for Cirque du Soleil today.

The generational hunger for the outside world that Dupéré represented became a fevered appetite by the 1960s, when so many of Dupéré's peers came of age.

FRONTISPIECE/
A PERFORMANCE AT **LA FÊTE FORAINE**,
A PRECURSOR TO CIRQUE DU SOLEIL,
BAIE-SAINT-PAUL, 1983.

01/
SAINT-URBAIN, CHARLEVOIX, IN RURAL
QUEBEC WHERE CIRQUE DU SOLEIL
WAS BORN, 1982.

02/
LES ÉCHASSIERS DE BAIE-SAINT-PAUL,
ANOTHER PRECURSOR TO CIRQUE,
PERFORMS IN QUEBEC CITY, 1983.

"QUEBECOIS PEOPLE ARE CLOSE TO THE EARTH. THAT MADE US INVENTIVE AND TURNED US INTO STORYTELLERS."

03/

04/

05/

THE SPIRIT OF EXPO 67

To many, Expo 67—the 1967 Universal Exposition in Montreal dubbed *Man and His World*—represented everything the period stood for.

Michel Crête is the influential set designer behind a number of Cirque shows. According to Crête, "You can trace the roots of Cirque du Soleil right back to Expo 67. The cultural wave that we were part of had its roots in that time. It was a gestating period."

"I think Expo 67 woke people in Quebec up," he says. "There was a meeting with the world that got everything started. It featured music most people had never heard, types of shows people had never seen, types of cuisine most people had never tried."

"There were a lot of young people from here who met young people from elsewhere," Crête continues, "and it gave us a taste for the world, a taste for creativity, a taste for demonstration."

Expo 67's message infused the spirit of the times: we are all citizens of one world, and, in that world, anything is possible. The world can be reimagined, and reinvented, for the better.

"EXPO 67's MESSAGE INFUSED THE SPIRIT OF THE TIMES: WE ARE ALL CITIZENS OF ONE WORLD, AND, IN THAT WORLD, ANYTHING IS POSSIBLE. THE WORLD CAN BE REIMAGINED, AND REINVENTED, FOR THE BETTER."

COMMUNES AND COOPERATIVES

The changes of the 1960s led directly to the forming of communes and cooperatives throughout Quebec. These became fertile breeding grounds for the growing street performer scene that would nourish, enrich, and build a foundation for Cirque du Soleil.

The two men who would have the greatest influence on Guy Laliberté in Cirque's early years—Gilles Ste-Croix and Guy Caron—were both active in the commune and cooperative network.

Gilles Ste-Croix, one of Cirque du Soleil's first artists and its artistic director throughout the 1990s, was born in a small Quebec town with a population of only 3,000. He first became active in communes in his twenties, on Canada's West Coast, where he was swept up by the spirit of the counterculture. "I wanted to be in show business," he explains, "but my parents had said: 'No way, anything else.' So I ended up on the West Coast, in Vancouver. I realized there was a whole movement I could be part of. I lived with these freaks, trying to make a change in society. Vancouver was really influenced by the West Coast, San Francisco. Lots of draft dodgers were coming up and bringing their culture, their political fight. It was a maelstrom."

By the mid-1970s, Ste-Croix returned to Quebec, establishing himself within a network of communes that extended across rural Quebec. "I ended up in this really politically oriented commune," he recalls. "We were trying to be self-sufficient and ecologically sound. You couldn't bring a guitar in unless it was for everyone! It was very socialist in orientation."

The rural communes were connected to cooperatives in Montreal, part of what Ste-Croix describes as "a network working together to create an alternative economy." In Montreal, he adds, "you could really feel the counterculture scene growing."

One of these cooperatives was a café called La Grande Passe. Among its many directors was actor, clown, and street performer Guy Caron. Caron would eventually become Cirque du Soleil's first artistic director. In the mid-1970s, he was busy mounting exhibitions and performances. These turned La Grande Passe into an experimental meeting place for street performers, clowns, actors, and aspiring folk musicians—among them a teenage accordion player whose name was Guy Laliberté.

06/07/
La Fête Foraine, 1983.
A gathering of street performers,
it was inspired by the communal
spirit of the 1960s.

07/

GUY LALIBERTÉ

Guy Laliberté, born in 1959, was only a child when Expo 67 and the hippie culture of the 1960s made contact with Quebec. Nevertheless, the movement that resulted was still in full swing in the mid-1970s, when Laliberté first decided to become involved in show business as a sixteen-year-old high school student.

It happened at a concert by Cajun musician Zachary Richard. Richard, from Louisiana, was featured at a French folk-music festival in Montreal's Lafontaine Park. "I had been interested in folk music since I was fourteen," explains Laliberté. "I come from a musical family. My father played accordion, we all sang."

Laliberté describes his "Eureka!" moment this way: "Zachary Richard was headlining the Quebec-Louisiana night. He was great. And during the show, he extended an invitation to the audience. He said: 'You should come down to Louisiana and celebrate Mardi Gras with us!' The next day, I thought: 'Okay, I'll do it!'"

Richard's invitation came at a propitious moment in Laliberté's life. A high school drama teacher by the name of Pierrette Brunelle had been nurturing his innate interest in performance and spectacle. "Pierrette was an important person in my life, I would say the first adult who ever had an influence on me that way," Laliberté recalls today.

Richard's stage banter planted an idea in Laliberté's mind that would allow the teenager to combine his growing love of show business with a deep-seated interest in travel, and a natural flair for promotion and production. Laliberté set out to organize a school trip to the Cajun heartland of Louisiana.

At this point in his life, Laliberté had already been the driving force behind a handful of high school events. However, he calls the Louisiana trip his first "real challenge," explaining: "Everything I'd organized up until then was part of a preexisting structure, but this was the first thing I had to do from scratch. I had to get permission from parents and school, I had to raise funds. I had to organize the whole thing. We raised money through benefit shows, flea markets, garage sales, however we could."

Laliberté enlisted Pierrette Brunelle to help him. He also turned to another early mentor: Gilles Garant. "Gilles Garant was a folk musician on the Montreal scene, and he was another major influence on me," Laliberté says. "He was the first guy to really teach me about the importance of being socially aware and engaged, and committed to doing things to enact positive change. Also, he'd been to Louisiana already, which was a plus."

The experience gave Laliberté a profound feeling of accomplishment: they were able to get the financing they needed, and had a little money left over in the bank.

Laliberté's love of folk music eventually brought him into contact with Guy Caron and the emerging artists at La Grande Passe. "I was really influenced by that whole scene," he says, "Guy Caron and those guys—I hung around them. I was the whippersnapper in the group. They were all five, ten years older than me. They were principally street performers, but they were also into the Quebec folk-music scene."

After high school, Laliberté became involved with a folk group called La Grande Gueule (Big Mouth): "I played the accordion and the harmonica, and I sang." Music gave Laliberté his first real taste of the road: "We played around the province, at festivals. Some of the guys were working, so when they couldn't make it, I'd go alone, from festival to festival, from hostel to hostel."

Thus began a life of travel and performance that would, in a short time, lead him directly to Gilles Ste-Croix, and the forming of an embryonic theater group that would become Cirque du Soleil in 1984.

08/
Guy Laliberté clowns with friend Pierre Lachapelle and mentor Gilles Garant on the school trip he organized to Louisiana, his first "real challenge," 1976.

09/
Guy Laliberté on his first tour of Europe as a street entertainer, 1978.

09/

CHAPTER 2

PRECURSORS

THE EXPERIENCE OF QUEBEC STREET PERFORMERS IN THE 1960s AND 1970s EVENTUALLY LED TO THE CREATION OF THREE COLLECTIVES THAT, TOGETHER, FORMED THE NUCLEUS OF CIRQUE DU SOLEIL.

GILLES STE-CROIX AND THE BREAD AND PUPPET THEATER

For Gilles Ste-Croix, the idea of incorporating circus skills into theatrical performance came directly out of his experience in communes. "I was in a commune in a place called Victoriaville, Quebec, which is very close to Vermont," he says. "We were just trying different things and, one day, we were picking apples in the orchard. I thought: 'Wouldn't it be great if the ladder was attached to my legs?' So I decided to make a pair of stilts." An American in the commune saw what Ste-Croix was doing and asked, "Do you know there are people in Vermont who do theater on stilts?"

The people in question were The Bread and Puppet Theater, an experimental theater troupe/protest group founded by German expatriate Peter Schumann.

"Bread and Puppet was a commune, and they made a living partly from doing shows," Ste-Croix explains. "They were a real product of the 1960s. Schumann had come over from Germany and built a theater show using big puppets, to protest the Vietnam War."

"They started The Big Revival Circus using all kinds of animals made of papier-mâché. They'd do circus shows every year, and they would invite groups to come and play. My initial reaction was, 'Wow! This is fantastic!' I heard that they were giving classes in different cities, and I said, 'I want to be part of that!'"

Ste-Croix eventually became friendly with Schumann, who asked him to take part in a Bread and Puppet Theater show. "He needed a stilter," Ste-Croix recalls. His brief experience (one performance) planted a seed: "I thought, 'This is what I want to do! Why can't we do this in Quebec?'"

02/

"I THOUGHT, 'THIS IS WHAT I WANT TO DO! WHY CAN'T WE DO THIS IN QUEBEC?'"

01/
GILLES STE-CROIX, A FORMATIVE
INFLUENCE ON CIRQUE DU SOLEIL,
ON STILTS, 1981.

02/
LA FÊTE FORAINE, BAIE-SAINT-PAUL,
1982.

03/
GUY CARON CLOWNS AROUND, 1984.
THE FOUNDER OF THE NATIONAL CIRCUS
SCHOOL, HE WAS CIRQUE DU SOLEIL'S
ARTISTIC DIRECTOR FROM 1985
TO 1988.

03/

GUY CARON AND THE NATIONAL CIRCUS SCHOOL

In the meantime, in Montreal, Guy Caron, one of the founders of La Grande Passe café, had decided to delve more deeply into the world of the circus. Caron was performing as a clown in a trio called *Chatouille et Chocolat* (Tickles and Chocolate). "Chatouille" and "Chocolat" were played by Sonia Côté and Rodrigue Tremblay, respectively—both actors now well known in Quebec circles. ("I was the 'et,'" explains Caron dryly.) Chatouille et Chocolat earned the respect of their fellow street performers when they got accepted to a circus school in Hungary in 1974. According to Gilles Ste-Croix, "Everybody in Quebec was saying, 'They made it!'"

While enrolled in the Hungarian program, Caron immersed himself in circus artistry from around the world. "We saw lots of circuses," he remembers, "maybe two every three weeks."

He was a quick study, completing the twenty-four-month program in only eleven months. "Our act was more experienced than a lot of the other students," Caron says, "and I thought we would learn more if we came back to Montreal and created our own school, bringing together the artists we already knew from places like La Grande Passe."

He returned to Montreal with the goal of founding Canada's first national circus school. By 1981, he succeeded, setting up shop in a free space offered to him by a friendly priest, Marcel de la Sablonnière, at a community center called the Centre Immaculée Conception, in Montreal's East End. The École Nationale de Cirque, or the National Circus School, was born.

In years to come, the National Circus School—while never officially affiliated with Cirque du Soleil—would be plumbed as a source for many of Cirque du Soleil's artists and trainers, particularly during Cirque's early years.

04/

COMING TOGETHER: LE BALCON VERT AND BAIE-SAINT-PAUL

By 1979, Gilles Ste-Croix had moved to Baie-Saint-Paul, an artist's colony near Quebec City. He had been hired to manage Le Balcon Vert, a youth hostel that was to open in the summer. Among other duties, he would be in charge of entertainment, organizing events and activities for young travelers. It was during a visit to Le Balcon Vert that Guy Laliberté first met Gilles Ste-Croix.

Laliberté had toured Europe as a folk musician, and experienced the world of street performers. "I played in the street," he explains, "and in Paris, I met up with acrobats and fire-breathers. Street performers and folk musicians were kind of on the same circuit."

By the time he returned to Canada in 1979, Laliberté had become a fire-breather. Once home, his goal was to generate enough funds to leave again and ply his new trade on beaches in Florida or Hawaii. He landed a job on a major hydroelectric project in James Bay, but his time on the project was ultimately cut short by a workers' strike. Having heard about the street performers and artists gathering around Le Balcon Vert, he headed to Baie-Saint-Paul.

Laliberté's goal was to offer the youth hostel his services as an entertainer, in exchange for food and lodging. "They wouldn't have to pay me," he points out, "since I had unemployment insurance. I

thought, 'When the strike's over, I'll go back to James Bay.' Traveling down from James Bay, Laliberté arrived in Baie-Saint-Paul at night, only to discover that Le Balcon Vert had not yet opened its doors for the season. "It was still early in the season," Laliberté explains, "so people were only just arriving, looking for work."

As he stood by the closed hostel, a group of people approached, among them Gilles Ste-Croix and Daniel Gauthier, a fellow student from Laliberté's high school. "I knew Daniel, though we weren't friends exactly (that came later). He was acting as a kind of administrator/accountant for Le Balcon Vert. It was the first time I met Gilles," says Laliberté. "I made them my offer," he continues, "and they said 'yes'. Over the next month or so, we became friends and set up Le Balcon Vert for the season together. I always thought I'd be going back to James Bay at any moment, but the strike lasted all summer."

Daniel Gauthier would go on to become Cirque du Soleil's chief administrator, and Laliberté's partner from 1987 to 2001.

Gilles Ste-Croix's influence on Guy Laliberté and the founding of Cirque du Soleil would be enormous. Ste-Croix jokingly puts it this way: "I always say Guy Laliberté founded Cirque du Soleil, but I founded Guy Laliberté. He's the father of Cirque. I'm the grandfather."

04/
LES ÉCHASSIERS DE BAIE-SAINT-PAUL
PERFORM LE DÉFILÉ DU DRAGON, 1981.
PERFORMERS INCLUDE, FROM LEFT TO
RIGHT: GILLES STE-CROIX (ON
STILTS),GUY ARSENAULT, LORRAINE
POTVIN, JOSÉE BELANGER, GUY
LALIBERTÉ (BREATHING FIRE), AND
SERGE ROY (IN WHITE SUIT).

05/
JOSÉE BÉLANGER, A PERFORMER WITH
LES ÉCHASSIERS DE BAIE-SAINT-PAUL,
IN MAKEUP, 1982.

Laliberté finds the formulation amusing, but rejects it, saying instead that he and Ste-Croix were "great friends," and "close collaborators" who built a dream together.

In the summer of 1979, the dream in question was Ste-Croix's. Ste-Croix introduced Laliberté to the idea of turning the talent congregating at Le Balcon Vert into a troupe that would perform theater on stilts, as The Bread and Puppet Theater had done.

The dream began to take shape over the winter of 1979-1980. "A bunch of us decided that we wanted to take a shot at keeping Le Balcon Vert open over the winter," remembers Laliberté. "We lived there: me, Serge Roy, Pino Noel, who was a clown, and Stéphane Roy, who eventually became the Set Designer for *Dralion*, *Varekai* and *Zumanity*."

Ste-Croix, who was living away from Le Balcon Vert with his wife and family, continued to bond with Laliberté. "That winter, we hatched yet another plan," recalls Laliberté. "There was a federal election, and I ran as a candidate for the Rhinoceros Party, as Guy "Pantoufle" ("Slippers") Laliberté. Gilles was my campaign manager." The Rhinoceros Party, a registered Canadian political party from 1968 to 1993, was devoted to "creative anarchy."

Its platform promises over the years included:
- repealing the law of gravity
- paving over the province of Manitoba to create the world's largest parking lot
- instituting illiteracy as Canada's third official language
- tearing down the Rocky Mountains so Albertans could enjoy the sunset on the Pacific coast
- building sloping bicycle paths across the country so that Canadians could "coast from coast to coast"
- turning Montreal's rue Ste-Catherine into the world's longest bowling alley
- painting Canada's coastal sea limits so Canadian fish could know where they were at all times and banning Canadian winters.

During the same period, Gilles Ste-Croix, working with a partner called Sylvain Néron, officially founded the Quebec-based troupe that would perform theater on stilts. St-Croix and Néron called it Les Échassiers de Baie-Saint-Paul (The Stilt-Walkers of Baie-Saint-Paul). Their first production would be *La Légende d'Alexis le Trotteur*, a play about a Quebecois folk hero. With performers and crew culled from his friends and street performers from Montreal at Le Balcon Vert, the only thing he needed was money.

06/

06/
CIRQUE FOUNDER GUY LALIBERTÉ ONSTAGE AS LE PÈRE MALTAIS, A CHARACTER IN **LES ÉCHASSIERS DE BAIE-SAINT-PAUL**'S PRODUCTION OF *LA LÉGENDE D'ALEXIS LE TROTTEUR*, 1981.

07/
ÉCHASSSIERS ONSTAGE (GILLES STE-CROIX ON STILTS, BACKGROUND; DANIE FRENETTE AND CARMEN RUEST, FRONT).

07/

GILLES STE-CROIX AND THE ISLAND OF THE IMMORTALS

In the spring of 1980, Ste-Croix applied to the Quebec provincial government for funds. "There was funding available, because the Parti Québécois government had allotted a lot of money to push Quebec culture," he explains. However, his plan was met with initial skepticism: "The guy who read the project said, 'Well, you need endorsement, you're nobody.' And I said, 'Yeah, but I'm serious. I can have the mayor of Baie-Saint-Paul endorse this.'"

Faced with resistance, Ste-Croix decided that performing a stunt would be necessary to convince the government that he was, indeed, somebody. "I told all the businesses in Baie-Saint-Paul that I would walk from Baie-Saint-Paul to Quebec City on stilts—fifty-six miles," he recalls, his delight still evident. "They had seen me walking on stilts in the streets, they knew I could do it. I asked for a certain amount of money per mile. I had a camera film me, and a truck following me. It took twenty-two hours."

The difficulty of the walk, and the beauty of the surroundings, led to a visionary experience. "Baie-Saint-Paul is by the Saint Lawrence River," he explains, "and, as you go up toward Quebec City, you rise maybe four thousand feet. You go over these rolling hills, high up. And during that day and night, I caught what [psychedelic author] Carlos Castaneda calls 'the bird eye.' I could see like a bird! In Castaneda, Don Juan says: 'If you catch the bird eye, you can see far,' which means you can see the future!"

As he walked, Ste-Croix remembers, his recollections from reading Castaneda mingled with other memories. "I remembered something I'd read in *The Book of Symbols*," he says, "back when I started to walk on stilts. There was a saying in there by Lao-Tzu: 'He who walks on stilts can be compared to the White Crane of China, and no mountain or river can stop him from attaining the Island of the Immortals.'"

Ste-Croix came to a gleeful conclusion: "It was fantastic! There I was: I'd caught the bird eye, and I felt like the White Crane flying to the Island of the Immortals. And I think today, I could die, but what I have accomplished, and what Cirque du Soleil has become, is from that walk. We touched the Island of the Immortals!"

He describes the walk as "a rite of passage." "I wanted to become a showbiz person, but I had to have a trial by fire to do it. And that walk was like the shaman going into a sweat lodge to get his vision. I walked for twenty-two hours on stilts to get my vision. And after that, I was indestructible. I could do anything!"

08/
GILLES STE-CROIX ON HIS HISTORIC STILT
WALK FROM BAIE-ST-PAUL TO QUÉBEC
CITY, 1980. STE-CROIX UNDERTOOK THE
WALK TO RAISE THE FUNDS NECESSARY
FOR THE FORMATION OF LES ÉCHASSIERS
DE BAIE-SAINT-PAUL.

08/

LES ÉCHASSIERS DE BAIE-SAINT-PAUL: FIRST STEPS

The walk had the immediate effect of persuading a reluctant bureaucracy to fund his project. "At the end of the walk," Ste-Croix recalls, "we made sure *Le Soleil*, Quebec City's newspaper, took pictures. I ended up on the front page. So the bureaucrat who received my application receives the *Soleil* and thinks 'This guy's crazy!' He called me and said, 'Well, if you did this, you proved you can do the project.'"

"I hired people for costumes, to direct the show, and performers. Everyone got a job for twelve weeks."

Laliberté returned to Baie-Saint-Paul to perform with Les Échassiers. The troupe toured Quebec throughout the summer of 1980, performing *La Légende d'Alexis le Trotteur,* and entertaining in the street. However, while they met with enthusiastic audience response, Laliberté says, "Les Échassiers lost money."

During the fall of 1980 and winter of 1981, Laliberté flew off to ply his trade in Hawaii, and Ste-Croix mitigated the losses from Les Échassiers' first year by setting up a nonprofit holding company called Le Club des talons hauts (The High-Heeled Club). By the summer of 1981, Les Échassiers de Baie-Saint-Paul were touring again, this time with Laliberté as both performer and tour manager.

Serge Roy, another member of the Balcon Vert gang and a performer with the Échassiers, remembers the working relationship between Ste-Croix and Laliberté in those days this way: "Guy was always the go-getter, the person who knocked on doors. He had balls of steel. Gilles Ste-Croix was the ringleader, the catalyst." (Roy, who is still with the company, would eventually become Cirque du Soleil's first tour manager, and then its stage manager, as well as the artistic director of many of its shows.)

In 1981, the group added an act to their repertoire called Le Défilé du Dragon (The Dragon Parade), featuring a large puppet operated by seven people. Ste-Croix, Laliberté, and their friends came full circle when they played at The Bread and Puppet Theater during that summer's tour. "Peter Schumann came up to see me," says Ste-Croix, and he said, 'Wow!' He really liked it."

By the end of the 1981 season, Les Échassiers de Baie-Saint-Paul broke even. Its success would inspire Laliberté, Ste-Croix, and company to organize a street performance festival, which could be considered Cirque du Soleil in embryo. It was called La Fête Foraine.

09/

LES ÉCHASSIERS DE LA BAIE

Sont une troupe de théâtre qui se produit en spectacle, il va sans dire, sur échasses…

A l'automne 1979, une subvention du Conseil des Arts au programme exploration ainsi que le programme Ose-Arts du gouvernement québécois, nous a permis de démarrer notre projet…

Plusieurs membres de notre troupe avaient déjà à leur actif des réalisations personnelles: participation au "Bread and Puppet" au Etats-Unis et au Québec, spectacles de clowns, d'acrobatie, d'équilibristes, de danses, de chants, de musique et d'avaleur de feu… Voulant concentrer cette énergie autour d'un thème se rattachant à une histoire singulière bien d'ici, il nous vint à l'idée de lier les échasses à la vie et à la légende d'Alexis le trotteur…

Les Échassiers sont maintenant en mesure de vous présenter, sur scène et à l'extérieur, un spectacle et deux animations après l'expérience concluante d'une tournée de plusieurs villes du Québec (Jonquière, Québec, Montréal, La Malbaie, La Grande Virée de Lachute, Baie St-Paul, Rimouski, Chicoutimi…

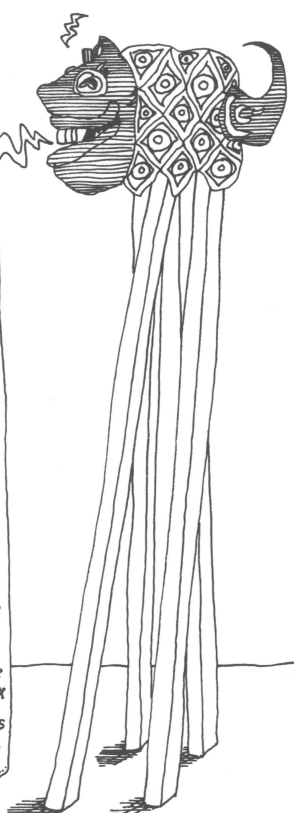

09/
Les Échassiers de Baie-Saint-Paul perform Le Défilé du dragon in Québec city, 1981.

10/
A poster advertising Les Échassiers de Baie-Saint-Paul. It describes the company's history and the inspiration for its first show, a Quebec folktale.

11/
Small-town crowds would gather at La Fête Foraine to be entertained and to take lessons in the circus arts.

12/
Carmen Ruest performs on stilts at La Fête Foraine, 1982.

11/

12/

13/

14/

LA FÊTE FORAINE

The first Fête Foraine took place in Baie-Saint-Paul in 1982. It was run by Le Club des talons hauts, whose first president was Serge Roy, and whose members included Gilles Ste-Croix, Guy Laliberté, and others. During their tours with Les Échassiers, Ste-Croix, Laliberté, and Roy had become enamored with the idea of establishing a street performer festival in Baie-Saint-Paul.

Foraine translates roughly as "carny," and the name Fête Foraine—rather than, say, "The Street Performer Festival"—was chosen out of necessity. "You actually couldn't do a 'festival' in Baie-Saint-Paul anymore," explains Gilles Ste-Croix wryly, "because they had had a folklore festival in the 1970s, and the bikers took over. It became a mess, so they voted in a bylaw

against festivals. So I said, 'We don't want to do a festival. We want to do a *fête foraine*. It's like what they used to do in the middle ages, when the minstrels came, and there was an exchange of crafts and so on." The choice of "fête" (celebration) made a crucial difference. "If I'd said 'a minstrel's festival,' we'd have been screwed, so we said *'fête foraine',* and explained that *'foraine'* meant 'street performers.' They said 'Okay.'"

Le Club des talons hauts envisioned the festival as the second of two ongoing projects under its banner. The first, Les Échassiers de Baie-Saint-Paul, would continue to tour under Ste-Croix's guidance. Guy Laliberté became General Manager of La Fête Foraine.

13/14/
SCENES FROM **LA FÊTE FORAINE**,
1983.

15/
ORIGINAL LOGO DESIGN FOR
LE CLUB DES TALONS HAUTS,
CIRQUE DU SOLEIL'S PARENT
COMPANY, BY JOSÉE BÉLANGER.
1982.

16/
JOSÉE BÉLANGER AND GUY CARON
ON STILTS AT **LA FÊTE FORAINE**,
1982.

15/

16/

17/

GUY LALIBERTÉ, PRODUCER

The first Fête Foraine took place in July 1982, and ran for a week. The second and third, in 1983 and 1984, ran for ten days. Guy Laliberté had become an impresario, bringing together talent from the street performer scene to entertain visitors to Baie-Saint-Paul under a colorful Big Top.

As well as performances, La Fête Foraine featured workshops in the circus arts for the public. At the end of La Fête Foraine's run, those who had taken part in the workshop could join the professional performers in a street performance.

To find artists who would be willing to guide the workshop's participants, Laliberté turned to his old friend Guy Caron, still active in Montreal with the National Circus School. Caron was hired as a performer, and supplied artists and teachers from his school.

René Dupéré, who had become a traveling street musician in the years leading up to La Fête Foraine, was among them, along with his street band La Fanfafonie. He would write music for the nascent circus even at this early stage.

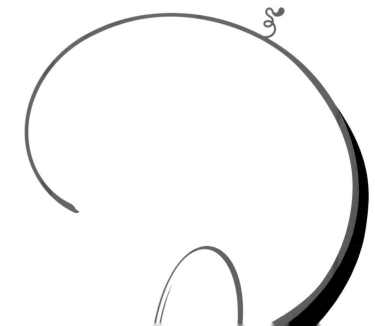

18/

"I'M CAPABLE OF FINDING A BALANCE BETWEEN BUSINESS AND CREATIVITY, AND SEEING HOW CREATIVITY CAN GROW OUT OF THAT BALANCE."

A HEAD FOR BUSINESS

La Fête Foraine project was a financial success. "We lost a little in the first year," explains Laliberté, "about ten thousand dollars or so. But we were able to absorb it in the second year." According to Gilles Ste-Croix, Guy Laliberté had decided to turn the cooperative, artistic venture into a moneymaker. "In 1982, admission was free. By 1983, it was: if you come onsite, you pay one dollar. We had a tent, and if you wanted to see the artists performing in there, you had to pay two dollars." Laliberté, ever mindful of details, corrects him: "It was five dollars, actually."

Guy Laliberté has been an artist since his youth, performing first as a folk musician, and later as a stilter and fire-breather. His creative vision, and his instinctual understanding of what audiences will respond to, has always driven Cirque du Soleil. From the beginning, however, his creativity has been complemented by a cool head for business. Serge Roy, who has known him since the early days, attributes this to Laliberté's parents: "His father had a good job, with Alcan, I think, but he also ran a business from home. His mother ran her own esthetician business. It was in his blood."

Laliberté concurs: "I had a business goal, always. I knew it took discipline to make things happen, even when I did projects at school. I think it's a quality I have: I'm capable of finding a balance between business and creativity, and seeing how creativity can grow out of that balance."

He adds that achieving that balance is impossible without the help and support of others. "Even at the very beginning, I had a lot of help. Daniel Gauthier was in charge of administration. Hélène Dufresne was my assistant. Jean David was Stage Manager, Richard Bouthillier was our Technical Director and, eventually our Tent Master, Josée Bélanger was in charge of Festooning, and Robert Lagueux was in charge of Communications. They were great."

17/
GUY LALIBERTÉ WITH DIABOLOS, 1983.

18/19/
GUY LALIBERTÉ PERFORMS IN THE STREET
AS A FIRE-BREATHER, 1982.

19/

20/
LA FÊTE FORAINE, 1983.

21/

INTIMATIONS OF CIRQUE

During La Fête Foraine's first two years, it occurred to Laliberté that he had the makings of a homegrown circus on his hands. "I remember we used to say: 'if we put all this under a Big Top and toured with it, we'd have a circus,'" remembers Gilles Ste-Croix today.

Laliberté would launch that circus the next year, in 1984, as part of the Quebec government's celebration of the 450th anniversary of French explorer Jacques Cartier's discovery of Canada. Laliberté would call it "Cirque du Soleil."

22/

21/
GILLES STE-CROIX, CARMEN RUEST AND
GEORGETTE RONDEAU ENTERTAIN, 1983.

22/
LOUIS BERGERON, A PERFORMER AT
CIRQUE DU SOLEIL'S FIRST SHOW, 1984.

23/24/
GYMNASTS NADIA COMANECI (ROMANIA)
AND NICOLAS ANDRIANOV (USSR) COM-
PETE AT THE 1976 SUMMER OLYMPIC
GAMES IN MONTREAL.

THE 1976 OLYMPICS,
AND THE INFLUENCE OF GYMNASTICS

"ONE OF THE THINGS THAT REALLY AFFECTED CIRQUE WAS THE 1976 SUMMER OLYMPIC GAMES IN MONTREAL. SUBLIMINALLY, IT INTRODUCED QUEBEC TO THE NOTION OF HIGH PERFORMANCE."

According to Lyn Heward, Cirque's President and Chief Operating Officer, Creative Content Division, the founding of the National Circus School at the Centre Immaculée Conception had a significant impact on the shape and form of what would eventually become Cirque du Soleil.

Heward is the former head of the Quebec Gymnastics Federation. She explains: "One of the things that really affected Cirque was the 1976 Summer Olympic Games in Montreal. Subliminally, it introduced Quebec to the notion of high performance. Nadia Comaneci came through here. So did Olga Korbut. High-performance sports like diving and gymnastics are a big part of our cultural heritage at Cirque, and I would say that what we saw in 1976 had an impact on the performance expectations of Quebecois."

Heward points out that Quebec gymnasts trained at the Centre Immaculée Conception. Years before Cirque du Soleil combined gymnastics and circus arts, gymnasts and circus artists were training together in one place. "There was a guy named Pierre Leclerc, who had competed in the Canadian Men's Team in 1976," she says. "He was involved in the National Circus School before Cirque started. He brought the notion of high performance into the mix back in the late 1970s and early 1980s." She cites André Simard as another example: "He was the head coach at the Centre Immaculée Conception when I arrived in Quebec in the early 1970s. And now, approaching sixty, he's with Cirque du Soleil."

"Right from the very beginning," she sums up, "there was a drive for high performance that met with and married street performance and circus performance."

CHAPTER
3

CIRQUE DU SOLEIL

IS BORN

➤ THE NAME **CIRQUE DU SOLEIL** CAME TO GUY LALIBERTÉ WHILE HE CONTEMPLATED HIS PROJECTS ON A BEACH IN HAWAII. "HAWAII," HE EXPLAINS, "WAS ALWAYS A CREATIVE PLACE FOR ME, A PLACE TO THINK. DURING THE WHOLE ÉCHASSIERS/FÊTE FORAINE PERIOD, I WAS REALLY ATTRACTED TO THE SUN. I SPENT A LOT OF TIME ON THE BEACH. WHEN I FIRST THOUGHT ABOUT FORMING A CIRCUS, I WAS WATCHING THE SUN SET ON A BEACH IN HAWAII."

LALIBERTÉ WAS ALSO INSPIRED BY SYMBOLOGY RELATED TO THE SUN. "THE SUN STANDS FOR ENERGY AND YOUTH," HE SAYS, "WHICH IS WHAT I THOUGHT THE CIRCUS SHOULD BE ABOUT."

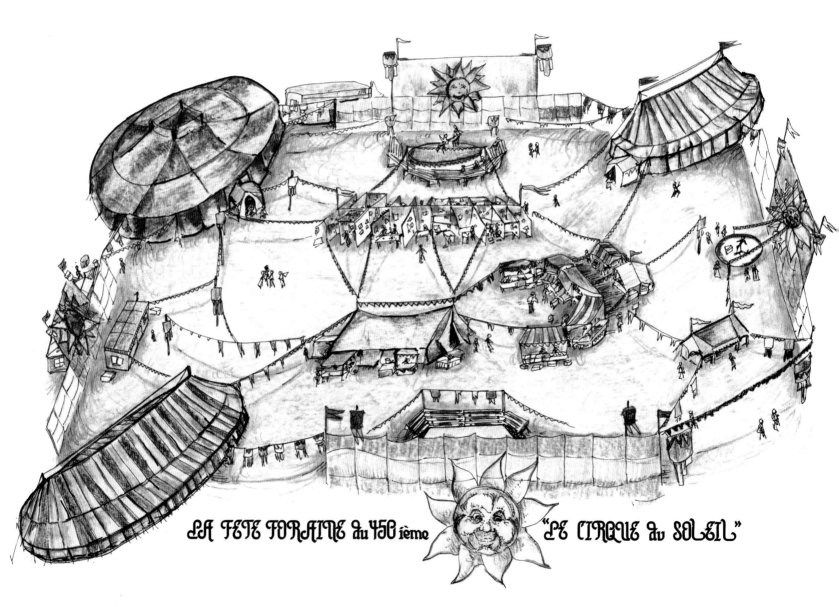

02/

03/

A ONE-YEAR PROJECT

At the very beginning, Cirque du Soleil was pitched as a one-year project. "With Les Échassiers, we played in Quebec City at Le Festival d'Été de Québec (the Quebec Summer Festival). Le Festival d'Été also had some joint programming with La Fête Foraine. We had become tight with the woman who ran it, whose name was Danielle Bouchard, "explains Laliberté. "She knew how successful we'd been with La Fête Foraine, and she introduced me to Jacques Renaud, who was with the 450th anniversary celebration's Commissariat général. He was the Director of Programming, and he was the one who gave us our first mandate: $30,000 to develop our Quebec circus concept."

"At the time," Laliberté continues, "she knew she was going to be in charge of Quebec's organizing committee for the International Year of Youth in 1985. She knew that we could probably do something under that umbrella, too, so she encouraged us to think about our proposal as a two-year project."

In the fall of 1983, Laliberté developed his ideas for Cirque du Soleil with a partner called Robert Lagueux, another member of Le Club des talons hauts, and a woman called Marguerite Fortin.

Lagueux had been in charge of Marketing for La Fête Foraine. "If you ask who founded Cirque du Soleil, I'd have to say it was me and Robert. Robert was a trumpet player who came out to Baie-Saint-Paul. He was Cirque's first Marketing Director. We really worked hand in hand at that stage."

For Laliberté, the plan that was eventually presented to Jacques Renaud was a compromise. "My dream was to put on a circus show under a big tent," he says, "but the government wanted an activity that would tour the regions. They didn't want a show, per se. They wanted animation, an impact that would be larger than just a show. So the compromise was to have this gathering of street performers descend on eleven towns over thirteen weeks. Within that, we'd have an opening and closing show—the embryo of what would become Cirque du Soleil."

For Laliberté, as creator, the show has always been the focus of his energies, his baby. While ever ready to talk about Cirque as a business, he is always thinking about how audiences will respond to his latest show. It is his greatest source of joy and pride. And from 1984 onward, when audiences responded enthusiastically to the new circus, it has also been the source of his achievements.

"There were also disagreements about how much money we could get," continues Laliberté. "We came back with a project that would cost $1.6 million, and Jacques Renaud said: 'But I've only got $900,000 for you. We can't spend more than that. But we pushed and cajoled him, and he eventually agreed to give us $950,000."

"But we still wanted that $1.6 million," adds Laliberté. "We did everything we could to get it. When we presented to the organizing committee, we had this nice color presentation that they loved. They said: 'Oh, we like that —how much will it cost?', and we said: '$1.6 million'. So they said: 'But we told you we've only got $950,000!' And we said: 'Oh, well we've got a presentation of what we can do for that,' and we pulled out a much less interesting presentation—in black and white. We went ahead with what was in the color presentation anyway, and, eventually, they kept giving us more and more, here and there, until we got our $1.6 million."

Despite the bargaining and compromises, Laliberté is very grateful for the early support he received at the birth of his dream. "The whole 450th Anniversary celebration was overseen by a man called Gilles Loiselle, and he really believed in us, too. If Danielle Bouchard, Jacques Renaud, and Gilles Loiselle hadn't been there at the start, we wouldn't be here today."

YEAR 1

In its first year, Cirque du Soleil was called "Le Grand Tour du Cirque du Soleil" ("Cirque du Soleil's Grand Tour"). It was one of two projects operating under the aegis of Le Club des Talons Hauts. The other was the third Fête Foraine. While Cirque du Soleil would tour the province throughout the summer, La Fête Foraine would once again take temporary residence in Baie-Saint-Paul. "In fact," points out Laliberté, "when Cirque du Soleil eventually got to Baie-Saint-Paul, we were both there at the same time. That was a beautiful moment for all of us."

With Robert Lagueux in charge of Marketing, old friends like Gilles Ste-Croix performing, and Laliberté running the show, Daniel Gauthier, who had been overseeing the finances at Le Balcon Vert, was brought in to act as an administrative controller.

CIRQUE'S FIRST TOUR MANAGER REMEMBERS BEING "TERRIFIED," AND RECALLS MISHAPS EVERY STEP OF THE WAY.

04/
CIRQUE DU SOLEIL'S FIRST BIG TOP, SHROUDED IN FOG. LEARNING TO LIVE WITH THE REALITIES OF RUNNING A TOURING CIRCUS (LIKE WEATHER) PROVED CHALLENGING.

LEARNING THE ROPES

While Cirque du Soleil generated great word-of-mouth around the province in 1984, the relative inexperience of its members made work difficult. Serge Roy, Cirque's first tour manager, remembers being "terrified," and recalls mishaps every step of the way. Trouble hit right from the start, while the new troupe rehearsed in Sainte-Thérèse. "The first time we put up the big top," Roy recounts, "we ended up damaging it a few hours before our first press conference."

"We'd hired a tent master from Switzerland and he didn't really know what he was doing," recalls Laliberté. "We were working all night to set up the tent before a busload of reporters were supposed to arrive from Montreal. By morning, we still hadn't finished, so I sent everyone off to rest a little. A couple of us stayed behind, and it just started pouring. You could see these big pools of water welling up on the tent, and we were thinking: 'oh no'." To Laliberté's horror, the big top's main mast crumpled under the extra weight.

"We'd been working so hard to be ready for the press conference," he says now, "and by the time the bus finally came, there was only one reporter on it!"

As it turned out, the nascent circus never had a dress rehearsal under the big top. After the first show in Gaspé, under a borrowed big top, Cirque du Soleil went on to play its second and third shows, in Baie-Comeau and Lac-St-Jean, in local arenas.

"The first *official* tent-raising, with our own tent, was only in Rimouski, the fourth stop on the tour," explains Serge Roy.

05/

EARLY CONFLICT

According to Guy Laliberté, learning how to work with a Big Top was only one of several problems he had to deal with. "Right at the start," he remembers, "there was a conflict with some of the artists on the tour. It was a 50/50 split between artists from Quebec and Canada, and artists from Europe and other places abroad. What I quickly learned was that the artists from abroad had a very different attitude to the project from ours. For the locals, we were building a home-grown circus, and we were ready to make sacrifices. For the Europeans, the tour was just a summer gig, a contract. They were mostly interested in getting paid and in getting the best working conditions possible."

"During the first stops on the tour," Laliberté continues, "they complained about everything. They kept telling us how inexperienced we were, how we didn't know what we were doing. It created such a bad atmosphere that we had to deal with an artists' rebellion in Gaspé, at the launch. The artists were supposed to be at our first press conference. Unfortunately, we had a tight budget. And there was a lack of lodging in Gaspé at the time, because that's where they were launching all of the festivities for the 450th anniversary — so most of the available rooms had been taken up by public officials. As a result, the only place where we could lodge all of them was at youth hostels in Gaspé. They took

umbrage at that. So I was standing there waiting for them at the press conference, and Gilles Ste-Croix walked up to me and said he had a letter from the artists that they wanted him to read to the press. I said 'no way, give me that', and saw that it was a list of complaints about how they're being treated. We had to bluff our way through the press conference without them."

Cirque's first shows took place in an atmosphere of mounting tension between artists and management. "It got really heated," remembers Laliberté. "People were making threats, almost getting physical. At one point, Robert Lagueux showed up with a baseball bat at our weekly production meeting with the artists." Things became so rough that Laliberté considered throwing in the towel. "I thought I was doing something noble," he explains, "bringing legitimacy to the whole street performer scene. The last thing I expected was that the artists would turn on me. I thought they were trying to squeeze us for what little we had. I almost thought: 'Forget it, you just don't get it. It's not worth it. But sheer pride kept me going. I thought 'You're not going to get the better of me.'"

Laliberté remembers Cirque's first official tent raising as the turning point in the struggle. "By the time we finally had our Big Top in Rimouski, our supposed 'Tent Master' from Europe just kept saying how it couldn't be put up, how it wouldn't work. So Jean David, Robert Lagueux, some technicians, and me said 'forget it man, we'll do it ourselves.' It wasn't easy, but we did it. And as soon as we had the big top up, I remember the artists coming in and looking around. I could see by the looks on their faces that they were thinking: 'Wait a minute, maybe we've got something here.'"

"Once they were won over, and once it became obvious how successful we were with audiences, the artists from abroad started to be won over, too. I remember a South American artist called Juan Saavedra saying, at the end of the tour, how great it was to be there at the beginning of something like Cirque du Soleil. We worked out our problems in the regions, and by the time we hit Quebec City and Montreal, we were firing on all cylinders."

PURSUING THE DREAM

Laliberté was ready to live with problems. Cirque du Soleil ended 1984 with $60,000 in the bank. Though the company had only received a one-year contract from the government of Quebec, Laliberté had a long-term vision for the company. "In 1984, I had already made a link, in my mind, with 1985, which was going to be the International Year of Youth," he says. "The idea was to sell Cirque as a two-year project." If problems were encountered in 1984, that was O.K.: "I always thought that 1984 would be the year we learned our circus ropes."

Unfortunately, while Canada's federal government was ready to offer funding for Cirque's second year, the Quebec provincial government was less than forthcoming. Luckily for the continued existence of the company, Quebec's Premier at the time, René Lévesque, intervened on Cirque's behalf.

"Danielle Bouchard, from the Quebec Festival, was close to Mr. Lévesque. We also had a good relationship with Marie Huot and Lynn-Sylvie Perron, who were his political attachées," recalls Laliberté. "We'd met them through Danielle Bouchard from the Quebec Festival. They introduced us to Mr. Lévesque. He was a big fan, and he personally twisted a few arms to get us the funding we needed from the Quebec government for 1985, as part of the Year of Youth." Lévesque's intervention led to a relationship with Laliberté that the latter remembers fondly. "It was at the end of his time as leader, close to the end of his life, actually," remembers Laliberté. "And during that period, I would see him as much as I could. He said something very nice about us in his memoirs. He cited us as an example of a new generation of Quebecer, people who wouldn't be hampered by the inferiority complex so many of us have been stuck with in the past."*

Even with Lévesque's help, however, securing funding from the Quebec government was not easy. "We were meeting constant resistance from Clément Richard, who was the Minister of Cultural Affairs. Richard was using us as a bargaining tool with Mr. Lévesque. He would say: 'If you want funding for Cirque, you have to give money to such and such a project first.' It became so contentious that we actually served Clément Richard a 'cease and desist' order at one point." The letter was delivered to the minister's office by a clown carrying balloons.

With funding from both the provincial and federal governments, Cirque du Soleil would survive another year. From 1985 on, Cirque would no longer be a traveling street performer festival. It would be a proper circus. In Laliberté's words, Cirque could now "meet its destiny head-on, without compromise."

* In a book called *Lévesque/Bourassa. Au delà de l'image: bilan 1970-1985*, published in 1985 by Les Éditions Québec/Amérique, Lévesque writes: "In this heartless world, which is becoming a small village, no one will have time for the people who drag their feet. As the Americans say, it will be time to put up or shut up. The only things we'll have a right to are the things we've truly worked for, and deserve." Later in the book, Lévesque cites examples of Quebecers who have demonstrated a new attitude to adapt to the demands of a new time. "We're finally beginning to see the fruits of the superhuman effort Quebec put itself to in the middle of the 1960s, when it became aware of how dangerously underdeveloped its human capital was... No sector of activity is safe: Olympic champions, winners of cross-Canada Accounting examinations [and] the extraordinary Cirque du Soleil, that United Nations in miniature performing for the young of all ages, whose inventor and leader is only 25 well-lived years old."

CIRQUE COULD NOW "MEET ITS DESTINY HEAD-ON, WITHOUT COMPROMISE."

05/
CIRQUE DU SOLEIL'S FIRST PERFORM-
ANCE IN GASPÉ, QUÉBEC. THE ENGAGE-
MENT WAS PLAYED UNDER A BORROWED
BIG TOP.

06/
RENÉ LÉVESQUE, THEN QUÉBEC'S
PREMIER, WITH GUY LALIBERTÉ UNDER
CIRQUE DU SOLEIL'S CHAPITEAU,
1984. HE WAS AN INFLUENTIAL EARLY
SUPPORTER, AND FRIEND TO LALIBERTÉ.

CHAPTER 4

REIMAGINING
THE CIRCUS

➤ CIRQUE DU SOLEIL BEGAN ITS SECOND YEAR
BY ACQUIRING A LARGER GRAND CHAPITEAU.
THE ORIGINAL TENT HAD SEATED ONLY EIGHT
HUNDRED, "NOT ENOUGH," EXPLAINS GILLES STE-
CROIX, "TO BE FINANCIALLY FEASIBLE. SO GUY WENT
TO EUROPE TO GET A BIGGER TENT." LALIBERTÉ
ALSO HIRED LONG-TIME COLLABORATOR GUY CARON
AS CIRQUE DU SOLEIL'S FIRST ARTISTIC DIRECTOR.
ACCORDING TO LALIBERTÉ, CARON WAS ONE OF
THE PEOPLE IN QUEBEC WHO KNEW THE CIRCUS
TRADITION BEST. THE TWO ALSO SHARED A VISION:
"WE WANTED TO CREATE A CIRCUS IN QUEBEC."

THE CIRCUS: A BRIEF HISTORY

In his book *La Grande Histoire du Cirque* (Editions du Chène, Paris, 2002), circus historian Pascal Jacob traces the roots of the European circus back to the orchestras of ancient Greece. In Jacob's view, what we recognize as the circus today was formed over centuries. Influences on the circus tradition included medieval English mystery theater, farce, roving entertainment of all kinds, and commedia dell'arte (an Italian combination of mime, dialogue, tumbling, and acrobatics that has its roots in the masked comedy of Ancient Rome). Other influences include Elizabethan theater and the training and exhibition of exotic animals.

Over the centuries, the circus took on an aspect of pomp, with definite military overtones in its music and costumes. Jacob argues that the martial elements come from the fact that the circus also has roots in the formal riding and equestrian tricks practiced by mounted soldiers over centuries.

In fact, Jacob places the beginning of the modern circus in 1530, when Peter Tremesin, an English knight, rode straddling two horses for the amusement of King Henry VIII. By 1768, in a village close to London, the first modern circus was founded by Philip Astley, a demobilized cavalry officer.

By 1779, Astley built a theater in London called Astley's Amphitheatre Riding House, built around a circular performance area. By 1783, he built the first permanent circus theater in Paris. As the eighteenth century wore on, Astley inspired a growing number of imitators. By 1807, the Franconi family, in France, opened Le Cirque Olympique, marking the first time a show of its kind was called a "circus."

The circus left the ground and literally vaulted into the air in 1859, when a French gymnast named Jules Léotard introduced a precursor to the trapeze. The tights he wore would soon become ubiquitous in the trade and would bear his name.

By 1871, at the Brooklyn World's Fair, P.T. Barnum and his associates introduced the world's first three-ring circus. Eighteen years later, in 1889, the Barnum and Bailey Circus first performed in Europe.

The twentieth century ushered in electronic media of all forms, from film to radio and television. Though the circus tradition may have dipped below the radar, it continued to thrive. Many family circuses still performing today, like Switzerland's Cirque Knie, were founded in the early part of the century. In 1919, Vladimir Lenin nationalized the Russian circus, under the advice of his minister of culture. The Soviet circus toured western Europe for the first time in 1956.

By the 1970s, a number of "alternative" circuses, bent on shaking the traditions that had been built up over centuries, began to appear in Europe.

The Chinese acrobatic tradition has a history of its own, tracing back at least as far as Europe's. And like the European tradition, it had a powerful effect on the creative minds behind the new circus from Quebec.

CHINESE ACROBATIC TRADITION AND EUROPEAN TRADITION HAD A POWERFUL EFFECT ON THE CREATIVE MINDS BEHIND THE NEW CIRCUS FROM QUEBEC.

SOURCES OF INSPIRATION

Cirque du Soleil has always been guided by Guy Laliberté's creative instincts, and by the faith and trust he puts in his most important collaborators. In its early years, Laliberté shaped the new circus's direction closely with his artistic director Guy Caron, who, as the head of the National Circus School, was familiar with trends and developments in the international circus world.

"For me, a huge historical event in Cirque's evolution occurred in 1982, when the Circus of China, led by a woman called Lili Ping, came to Montreal," Caron says. "Her troupe came to the Maurice Richard Arena in 1982. It was only supposed to be there for three weeks, but they stayed two months. Why? Because people were blown away!"

Caron describes the show enthusiastically: "Their show was strong because the music was created from the beginning to the end, and was played by a band. The costumes were designed very specifically for the acts, and they were beautiful. The choreography was beautiful. I thought, 'Wow! This is a show!' We don't need horses, or animals, or any of that. It can be about physical performances linked together."

He points to the Moscow Circus as another influence: "The Russians were so strong. But, more than that, some acts told a little story from beginning to end."

In fact, Caron's list of influences is long and comprehensive, including Cirque Grusse (the national circus of France), and a woman named Annie Fratelinni. "She ran an Italian theater school," Caron explains, "and every year she would take the school on a three-month tour, with all these young people. The energy was so powerful! The shows weren't always good, but the ideas were there. And I thought, 'This is what I have to do, bring young people to the circus, this energy.'"

While other circuses impressed Caron and Laliberté with their cohesiveness of approach and theatricality, the German Cirque Roncalli impressed them with its ability to immerse audiences in a fantastic alternate reality. "A beautiful circus!" Caron exclaims. "When you entered their big top, you were brought right into this magical environment, right from the entrance. Guy [Laliberté] and I walked in and went, 'Wow!' We did our own take on it."

Their experience at the Cirque Roncalli convinced Caron and Laliberté to take a new approach to bringing acrobatic equipment on and off the stage, a fourth-wall-destroying experience by that point. "We wondered how to deal with bringing the equipment on and off the stage, like props in the theater, without breaking the flow for the audience. The Cirque Roncalli did it by putting one performer in with the technical crew. We decided to go further, by making all the artists do it." The result would have far-reaching repercussions: "It meant that the artists had to keep performing between acts, always sticking to a 'storyline.'"

Guy Laliberté is also very grateful for the early support offered to him by Switzerland's Cirque Knie, run by the Knie family. "In the early days, Guy Caron and I went around to a lot of other circuses, asking for advice. Cirque Knie were absolutely fantastic. They welcomed us and gave us all kinds of excellent advice. Whenever I had questions about how to tour with a circus, they were happy to answer them."

Cirque du Soleil's relationsip with Cirque Knie went even further in 1985. "At the time," recalls Guy Caron, "we realized that we needed help with the Big Top. What do you do when the wind comes up? How do you adjust? Technical questions like that... and our Tent Master at the time, Richard Bouthillier, suggested we contact Cirque Knie for help. So Knie sent us their Tent Master, who'd been with them for decades, for a week. His name was Marcel Rossell, he was French. After that, Richard would go over to Switzerland on a regular basis for more training from Monsieur Rossell."

In 1990, during Cirque's first foray into Europe, the idea of a collaboration was floated. "We thought we should do a show together," explains Guy Caron, "and one of the reasons was that the younger members of the Knie family saw they could benefit from using our more up-to-date sound and lighting technology. Guy Laliberté said 'yes', right away, because he was so grateful for their help through the years, and he wanted to honor that relationship."

The show, called Cirque Knie Presents Cirque du Soleil, directed by Caron, played to Swiss audiences in 1992, and featured Cirque du Soleil performances combined with Cirque Knie's traditional animal acts.

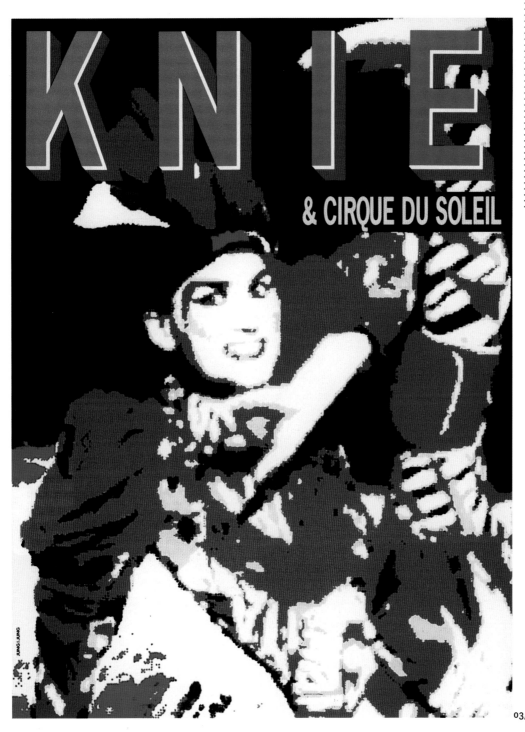

03/

01/
A POLISH CIRCUS POSTER FROM 1970
EVOKES THE ROOTS OF THE CIRCUS.

02/
JULES LÉOTARD, A CIRCUS ARTIST FROM
THE NINETEENTH CENTURY, AND INVENTOR
OF THE GARMENT THAT BEARS HIS NAME.

03/
A POSTER ADVERTISING CIRQUE DU
SOLEIL'S 1985 PRODUCTION WITH
SWITZERLAND'S CIRQUE KNIE, AN EARLY
INSPIRATION AND SUPPORTER.

04/
A CIRQUE DU SOLEIL PERFORMER MAKES
A DRAMATIC ENTRANCE, 1985.

FREE TO DREAM

From the very beginning, the creators at Cirque du Soleil felt free to explore uncharted territory. "We weren't part of the circus tradition, because we weren't a family," explains Gilles Ste-Croix. "Circuses in Europe were always run by families. If you weren't part of that family, you had no tradition, so you could do something different."

This feeling of freedom dovetailed neatly with Guy Laliberté's deep-seated conviction that Cirque du Soleil must embrace The New. "I believe that the more you give people something new," he propounds, "the more they'll like it."

To help them develop an innovative show in 1985, Laliberté and Caron turned to a director whose previous work had been with theater students: Franco Dragone.

FRANCO DRAGONE COMES ABOARD

Franco Dragone would become a major figure in Cirque du Soleil history, directing all of its shows up to, but not including, *Dralion*. Dragone, raised in Belgium, had been involved with the National Circus School since 1982, when Guy Caron had hired him to teach commedia dell'arte and acting techniques to his students.

"In 1984, when Cirque du Soleil got started, I wasn't with them," remembers Dragone. "I was doing a show with last-year students in Belgium that incorporated circus arts. In 1985, when Guy Caron had become artistic director, I think it was because of the work I had done with students that he asked me to direct the show. I said 'yes,' because I wanted to bring theater to the circus."

THE CIRCUS AS THEATER

Guy Caron confirms that making the circus more theatrical was a key goal. "It was important that we feel part of the circus world," he says, "but, at the same time, we wanted to change the way people did it, right from the start."

"We transformed the way you open the curtain inside the circus ring," he continues. "For the first time, we set up a camera so that the person opening the curtain could watch the action, and interact with it. The curtain became magic! We used the curtain as part of the show. And we put monitors backstage, so that the performers could feel more involved, so they could feel they were part of the show from beginning to end. They wouldn't just sit in their caravans waiting for their number."

Caron also saw a growing role for original music: "The music was part of the action. For us, music should create movement, and out of the movement should come music."

René Dupéré was hired to write the all-important music, as he had been in 1984. "In 1984, we used a lot of the stuff we had been playing as a street band for the show," he remembers. "We played a lot of Dixieland, some jazz, and I composed all the links between the numbers. But for the 1985 show, I composed about ninety-five percent of the music."

For Caron, establishing a cohesive presentation and a quasi-narrative, musical through-line set Cirque du Soleil apart. "To me," he says today, "the big secret of Cirque du Soleil is that we created shows like a film. We thought it should be edited and scored like film. If you take the music out, you don't have a Cirque du Soleil show. Cirque is like cinema: you edit it together to create drama, and to allow people to enter completely into the experience, like you do into a film screen. You enter into the experience, and forget everything else."

04/

A HISTORICAL ENCOUNTER

Speaking about his first encounter with Laliberté and company, Franco Dragone enthuses: "It was great! It's the kind of thing that happens once in your life."

Dragone remembers being deeply inspired by his new coworkers. "They didn't want a traditional circus," he says. "The first show that we did, we tried everything. I think the show lasted three and a half hours during our first run-through, because we had so much material, and so many people to do it. And they were all hungry to be in the show, to do something."

Dragone pushed them to explore the political, social, and artistic potential of increased theatricality. "I was listening to these street performers who were seeking some kind of respect for their work," he says, "and I was sure that we were on the cusp of some historical moment. In 1985 I remember telling everyone, 'You are not puppets. You are people with ideas, with something to say. You can't just be entertainers without having an idea of what's wrong with the world and taking a position on it!'"

"We had to develop and maintain our capacity for indignation," he continues. "Every day, you should feel indignant at some form of human misfortune or other." For Dragone, developing this capacity was essential to Cirque's evolution: "I think what made Cirque du Soleil different from other circuses was its desire to make a better life for people. The message behind every show is what makes Cirque different. It's not just entertainment, it's about life and what can make life more just. The humanity behind Cirque du Soleil is what makes the difference."

05/

"WHAT MADE CIRQUE DU SOLEIL DIFFERENT FROM OTHER CIRCUSES WAS ITS DESIRE TO MAKE A **BETTER LIFE FOR PEOPLE.**"

05/
FRANCO DRAGONE CONFERS
WITH ARTISTS.

06/
VARIOUS CHARACTER DESIGNS
BY DOMINIQUE LEMIEUX.
CIRQUE'S UNIQUE CHARACTERS
HAVE BEEN A DISTINGUISHING
FEATURE FROM ITS EARLY DAYS.

06/

A NEW APPROACH TO CHARACTER

One of Dragone's first contributions to Cirque was to train the 1985 artists in commedia dell'arte techniques. That, combined with his convictions about the potential of the theater to make an impact on the audience, had an immediate impact on character work within the circus. "We totally changed how to involve the characters at the very beginning of a show," explains Caron, "coming in with trench coats and commedia dell'arte masks.

"From the beginning I told them, 'I can't do the show unless I can bring life into the Grand Chapiteau. The characters we invent have to have something to do with life at large.' That's why the beginning of the first show I did had a crowd of people coming into the big top wearing trench coats. They take off their coats and transform themselves into circus artists."

Franco's contribution, while limited at first, would be extremely significant. For budgetary and scheduling reasons, Dragone wasn't involved in putting together the whole 1985 show, which was mostly overseen by Laliberté and Caron. "The structure of the 1985 show was still very conventional," explains Gilles Ste-Croix. "Franco just imagined a new beginning for the first act, and a beginning for the second act." Nevertheless, the simple gesture of transforming everyday people into circus artists—and therefore establishing a deeper connection between artist and audience—became a Cirque du Soleil trademark. "We've always used the same opening," smiles Ste-Croix, "whatever the show: people coming in from the street and becoming extraordinary."

The message of this opening gesture is clear and heartening. These artists, accomplishing incredible things, are people like us. We, too, can be extraordinary.

"THE CHARACTERS WE INVENT HAVE TO HAVE SOMETHING TO DO WITH LIFE AT LARGE."

07/

DEVELOPMENTS IN SET DESIGN

Just as some of its influences had done, Cirque du Soleil presented a show without animals in 1985. That simple fact allowed Cirque to innovate in terms of the design of its performance space. "In 1985, Cirque du Soleil became a typical one-ring circus like you see in Europe, but with no animals," explains Gilles Ste-Croix. "Because we had no animals, we didn't have to have a dirt floor. We could have a good, solid floor to do acrobatics and bicycle on... it was very simple, with nice, clean lines, a little Art Deco. The set could be a statement that we were different."

The fact that Cirque was different would be even clearer by their 1986 show. However, in order to make that show possible, Guy Laliberté would first have to wrestle with the company's near-crippling financial problems.

07/
A VIEW INSIDE THE GRAND CHAPITEAU.

08/
A REHEARSAL FOR *LE CIRQUE RÉINVENTÉ*.

09/
CIRQUE DU SOLEIL ORIGINAL STAFF, 1984.

08/

THE PIONEERS

IN CIRQUE DU SOLEIL'S FIRST YEARS, A TIGHT-KNIT GROUP OF
FRIENDS AND COLLABORATORS GAVE THEIR ALL TO MAKE THE DREAM
OF A QUEBEC-BASED CIRCUS A REALITY. "I CALL THEM 'THE
PIONEERS,'" SAYS GUY LALIBERTÉ, "THE PEOPLE WHO REALLY PUT
THEIR SHOULDERS TO THE GRINDSTONE WHEN WE WERE STARTING
OUT." LALIBERTÉ CREDITS THEM FOR THE PERSONAL SACRIFICES
THEY MADE: "THERE WAS NEVER ANY GUARANTEE THAT WE'D MAKE
IT, AND YET THEY WORKED HARD, FOR LONG HOURS, FOR NOTHING
AND MADE IT HAPPEN."

CIRQUE DU SOLEIL PIONEERS INCLUDE:

Josée Bélanger, Richard Bouthillier, Guy Caron, Jean David, Guy Devost, Hélène Dufresne, René Dupéré, Daniel Gauthier, Luc Lafortune, Robert Lagueux, Jean Laliberté, Anne Plamondon, Danny Pelchat, Serge Roy, Carmen Ruest, Guy St-Amour, Gilles Ste-Croix.

"While not 'pioneers' in the same sense, other employees have been with Cirque du Soleil for over ten years," adds Laliberté, "and we'd like to thank them for their valuable contribution, too."

These include:
Carmen Abad, Joseph Abramo, Maria Akhlatkina, Hélène Allard, Mario Allard, Stéphane Allard, René Arbour, Laurent Asselin, Sylvain Auclair, Marc Babin, Carole Baribeau, Julie Beaudoin, Lorraine Beauséjour, Linda Bélanger, Nathalie Bélanger, Julie Bennett, Georges Bertrand, Johanne Bérubé, Pawel Biegaj, Witold Biegaj, Alain Bigras, Claude Bigras, Yves Bigras, Bruce Bilodeau, Stacey Bilodeau, Robert Blain, Michèle Blais, Nathalie Bollinger, Robert Bollinger, Allister Booth, Jean-Paul Boun, Bernard Bowles, Lynn Bradshaw, Johanne Bricault, Jean-Francois Brissette, Debra Lynne Brown, Hélène Brunet, Brigitte Carbonneau, Cassera Michael, Lili Cauchon, Anna Chan, Paul Charlebois, Patrick Chassin, Ulziibayar Chimed, Gennady Chizhov, Nathalie-Cyd Clark, Jacques Cobetto, Stephane Cognac, Daniel René Cola, Pier Colbert, France Collins, Pietro Conforti, Warren-James Conley, Ann-Marie Corbeil, André Coté, Serge Coté, Vincent Cotnoir, Steve Cowart, Michel Crête, Alain Daigle, Joel Dallaire, Andrée Daneault, Mike Davies, Yves Décoste, Andrée Deissenberg, Michel Deschamps, Suzanne Desjardins, Luc Deslauriers, Francine Desrosiers, Brian Dewhurst, Nicholas Dewhurst, Franco Dragone, Magalie Drolet, Jennifer Dunne, François Dupuis, Linda Dupuis, Gaétan Durepos, Evelyne Durocher, Tamir Erdenesaikhan, Jeanette Farmer, Joanne Filion, Sylvain Forcier, Sonya Fortier, Suzanne Fournier, Kelly Frederick, Vincent Gagné, Marc Gagnon, Marie Gagnon, Richard Gagnon, Sylvie Galarneau, Nathalie Gauvin, France Gauvreau, Steve Gay, Johanne Gélinas, Line Giasson, Lucie Girouard, Yves Godcharles, Caroline Gosselin, Diane Goyette, Claude Gratton, Daniel Guillemette, France Guillemette, Sylvain Guimont, Marek Haczkiewicz, Ursula Haczkiewicz, Natasha Hallett, Pam Hanlon, Thomas Hanlon, Eric Heppell, Lyn Heward, Patrice Hollrah, Denis Horth, Richard Imbeau, Jinny Jacinto, Sean Jensen, Richard Joyal, William King, Vladimir Komissarov, Laurina Krommendijk, Louis Labelle, Marie-Josée Lachance, Carole Laflamme, Annie Lafontaine, Manon Lafontaine, Jocelyn Landry, Ginette Langevin, Chris Lashua, François Louis Laurion, David Lebel, Michel Leblanc, Paul Lecours, Lucie Legault, Céline Lemay, Jacques J. Lemelin, Dominique Lemieux, Denis Lepage, Andrei Lev, Nicolle Liquorish, Louise Marchand, Marco Lorador, Paulo Lorador, Linda Maffei, Stephen Manoogian, Christine Mariano, Margaret Frances Marks, Jacques Marois, Piotr Matula, Stéphane Mayrand, Peter Mcnaughton, Michael-Robin McRae, Manuela Medeiros, Adolfo Medel, Marie-Laure Mesnage, Éliane Miller, Lloyd Monteiro, Josée Montpetit, Gaetan Morency, Kirk Mortenson, Louise Murray, Carole Myles, Nicolette Naum, Kiki (Christine) Nesbitt, Alexey Novozhilov, Justin Osbourne, Walter van Osch, Damien Oxley, Hélène Painchaud, Jaque Paquin, Nathalie Parent, Pierre Parisien, France Paulin, Zdzislaw Pelka, Yves Pelletier, François Perron, Carl Perrotte, Mikhail Petrov, Pierre Phaneuf, François Pie, Émile Poulier, Janet Pundick, Benoit Quessy, Réjane Racine, Jean-Guy Rannou, Nathalie Renaud, Colombe Richard, Bruce Rickerd, Jack Ricks, Philippe Rivrais, Simon B. Robert, Danielle Rodenkirchen, Michael Rosenberger, Guennadi Rybine, Elena Santagata, Yannick Scullion, André Simard, François Simard, Mario Simard, Eligiusz Skoczylas, Marc Sohier, Claude Sonier, Teresa Soto, Alain Spooner, Gilles St-Amand, Luc St-Hilaire, Judith Stuewe, Monelle Sylvestre, Lance Taylor, Marie Tebbs, Denise Tétreault, Monique Therrien, Jean Thibault, Michel Thibodeau, Michel Thivierge, Todd Toresdahl, Chantal Tremblay, Hélène Tremblay, Line Tremblay, Mona Tremblay, Eleni Uranis, Christiane Vaillancourt, Mario Venditti, Boris Verkhovsky, Johanne Viens, Carolyne Vita, Andrew Watson, Mark Ward, Annie Wilkins, Eric Womack, Don Workman, Danny Zen.

"There have been others involved with us at some point over the years, like Normand Latourelle, Louise Roy, and Steve Zalac, whose presence we acknowledge," says Laliberté, "but these people were the ones who really made it happen."

NOTE: TRACKING THESE PEOPLE HAS BEEN A COMPLEX EXERCISE, AND IT IS POSSIBLE THAT SOME, REGRETTABLY, HAVE BEEN FORGOTTEN. WE APOLOGIZE FOR ANY OMISSIONS.

CHAPTER
5

GROWING PAINS

➤ **WHILE CIRQUE DU SOLEIL WAS MAKING ARTISTIC ADVANCES IN 1985, IT ALSO MET HEAD-ON WITH NEAR-FINANCIAL RUIN. THIS CRISIS TOOK ALL OF THE YOUNG COMPANY'S RESOURCES AND POWERS OF PERSUASION TO OVERCOME.**

"Nineteen eighty-five was very hard," recalls Guy Laliberté. "We had $60,000 at the end of 1984, but we committed to spending $1.6 million over 1985. We ended up running after money, and chasing our tails all the time. We had some government funding, but never the amount we needed, or when we needed it."

Fortunately, Laliberté did not have to deal with the administrative and logistical problems facing Cirque du Soleil alone. He had help from the beginning, from Daniel Gauthier. "Daniel worked with me. We shared the dream. He made a big contribution. He was totally involved. We shared responsibilities, and the job he had to do at the organizational and administrative level was as huge as the creative work I did."

"WE SHARED THE DREAM.

HE MADE A BIG CONTRIBUTION.
HE WAS TOTALLY INVOLVED."

MONEY TO THE RESCUE

Fortunately for Laliberté, Gauthier, and their fledgling company, La Caisse d'Économie des Travailleurs et Travailleuses du Québec, a member of Le Mouvement Desjardins, a Quebec-based Credit Union equivalent, offered financial support. Clément Guimond, who became their banker (and is still in that position at publication), recalls being persuaded by Cirque's passion and charm. In the documentary film *Run Before You Fly*, Guimond says: "If Guy Laliberté, Daniel Gauthier, and Gilles Ste-Croix walk into your office, you have no choice, if you're the slightest bit open to being passion-

ate about something. They can move in and win you over quickly. So part of it was the strength these young people had. The project was great, but they had no background. It was more the qualities of the people behind the project that made us sit down with them."

Clearly, the Laliberté/Gauthier team worked efficiently. According to Guimond: "They showed us not only that they had a dream, but that they could also deliver artistically. These people could turn a dream into concrete reality, and create something people wanted to see."

02/

"IN TORONTO, WE DIDN'T HAVE THE MONEY TO DO A PROPER MARKETING JOB. WE HAD A GOOD CRITICAL REACTION, BUT WE WEREN'T ABLE TO GENERATE THE WORD-OF-MOUTH WE NEEDED TO BE SUCCESSFUL."

THE NIAGARA FALLS DEBACLE

Cirque ran into financial problems in its first year when it expanded into markets outside of Quebec.

"It was part of our business plan to tour three places in the rest of Canada," explains Guy Caron. These included Ottawa, Toronto, and Niagara Falls. "But it didn't really work. There were maybe twenty-five percent capacity crowds. It was new to them, they didn't get it. They would send sports journalists to cover us!"

"In Quebec, things had gone fairly smoothly," specifies Laliberté. "But in Toronto, we didn't have the money to do a proper marketing job. We had cash flow problems, so we couldn't even buy ads in the newspapers. In Quebec, people knew who we were, so they would give us credit. But no one knew who we were in Ontario. We had a good critical reaction, but we weren't able to generate the word-of-mouth we needed to be successful." Cirque's failure to generate positive word-of-mouth during its first visit to Toronto didn't occur for lack of trying. Gilles Ste-Croix remembers walking through downtown Toronto on stilts, dressed in a monkey suit, in an effort to drum up publicity. One wonders what the unsuspecting motorists he stopped along the way thought of this odd apparition. Nevertheless, Toronto took little notice, and Cirque du Soleil soon ended up with a financial deficit.

The next stop, Niagara Falls, proved even more disastrous. "The Quebec Delegation had told us: 'We've got a place for you there, there are thousands of people who visit every year,'" recounts Laliberté. "But we didn't check it out, and that led to a Marketing 101 lesson for us. Sure, ten million people a year visit Niagara Falls, but the average visit is forty-five minutes long—not long enough to see a show!"

Serge Roy, who had become stage manager in 1985, remembers that so few people came out to see them in Niagara Falls, the artists made a rule: "If there were less people in the audience than were going to be onstage, we wouldn't perform."

Guy Caron sums up the result succinctly: "By the end of Year 2, we'd amassed a deficit of $750,000."

03/

04/

DEALING WITH ADVERSITY

"We were technically bankrupt," remembers Guy Laliberté. Yet he never lost faith in the future of his circus. For one thing, he knew he could count on gigs that had been booked for 1986 to tip back the scales, including Expo '86 in Vancouver. According to Laliberté, he could also count on two more things: "Public opinion, which was A-1, and really supportive suppliers."

A chief supporter was Clément Guimond and the Mouvement Desjardins. "In 1985," claims Laliberté, "they let about $200,000 worth of NSF [non-sufficient funds] checks go by. It was funny. First they would say, 'Okay, stop writing checks over $5,000!' So we'd pay, say, in increments of $1,000 or less. Then they'd say: 'No more checks over $1,000!', and so on. We ended up writing tons of checks for under $100! They took a big risk on us, much bigger than any other financial institution would have."

Daniel Lamarre, who is currently President and Chief Operating Officer at Cirque, was also a financer at the time. He, too, remembers finding Cirque persuasive: "I was at one of the largest public relations companies in Quebec. That's how I met Guy. He wanted to make some noise in the Montreal market. In the early days, Cirque couldn't pay our fee, because they had no money, but I accepted the job because what Guy was doing was so fantastic."

Laliberté and Daniel Gauthier worked hand in hand to stave off other unpaid suppliers. "We spent a month on the phone talking to people," he remembers. "Daniel took everyone under $5,000, I took everyone over, and we worked out deals."

The company needed bridge financing to last until 1986, and eventually the Quebec government's cultural arm offered to provide part of it. Surprisingly, Laliberté initially rejected the money. "We needed $400,000 to refinance, and they offered us $250,000. I could have taken it and paid some people off, but I turned it down. I said, 'You're making a bad financial decision. $250,000 isn't enough! It's either $400,000 or forget about it.' They would have ended up with a $250,000 loss. We knew we could make money. In fact, it turned out that our revenue projections were conservative."

01/
THE GRAND CHAPITEAU COMES DOWN IN OLD MONTREAL, 1984.

02/
DANIEL GAUTHIER AT WORK, 1984.

03/
NIAGARA FALLS, ONTARIO, WHERE CIRQUE LEARNED A DIFFICULT LESSON, 1985.

04/
A POSTER FOR CIRQUE'S 1986 SHOW, MAGIE CONTINUE.

CHAPTER
6

MOVING FROM

STRENGTH TO STRENGTH

➤ BY 1986, LALIBERTÉ WAS UNDER CRUSHING PRESSURE. HIS OLD ALLY, GILLES STE-CROIX, HAD DECIDED TO STOP PERFORMING AND MOVE ON. "I WAS THIRTY-FIVE AT THE END OF '85," HE RECALLS, "AND I WAS GETTING SORE." STE-CROIX LEFT CIRQUE DU SOLEIL TO EXPLORE OTHER OPTIONS, STUDYING THEATER AT CONCORDIA UNIVERSITY, AND FINDING EMPLOYMENT FOR A WHILE IN THE OPÉRA DE MONTRÉAL'S PROP WORKSHOP. YET, RATHER THAN RETRENCH, LALIBERTÉ DECIDED TO MOVE FORWARD ARTISTICALLY WITH CIRQUE DU SOLEIL'S 1986 SHOW.

MICHEL CRÊTE ARRIVES

Franco Dragone was once again hired to direct. This time around, he was joined by Michel Crête, with whom he would form an ongoing creative partnership. Crête—who would come to have enormous impact as Cirque's set designer—was originally asked to join as costume designer.

Initially, Crête was reluctant. "I really wasn't into the idea of designing costumes for a circus show at first," he remembers. "It's very demanding. When you design costumes for actors, it's one thing. They move from here to there, it's very simple. But circus performance makes all kinds of demands on costume designers, because of the extremes of movement. I thought it was a little much. So I said 'no' at first." Nevertheless, Caron and Laliberté eventually won him over.

To push the circus form further, Caron and Crête concentrated on altering the traditional approach to circus costumes. This was done, in part, to increase theatrical cohesiveness. "I thought that performers should be dressed in a coordinated manner, from beginning to end, like at the opera, or in a musical," Caron explains. "Before us, performers would just show up at a circus with whatever costume they had. We wanted to make it more theatrical. We wanted to make it more poetic."

Michel Crête seized the opportunity to try something new. "I'm not a circus specialist," he says today. "I hadn't done a lot of research into the circus tradition. That there was a tradition was obvious. That's what we wanted to shake up with our costume designs. In the traditional circus, there was always a reference to the military, to the equestrian tradition, stuff like that. It was easy to say, 'Let's try something else.'"

Crête points to military-themed costumes as an obvious starting point for change. "The military costumes made things seem so tight and rigid," he points out, "and I was seeing these young people pulling off incredible physical feats that were so free and unrestricted."

The inclusion of children in the show proved another source for inspiration. "In the nineteenth century," Crête says, "they used to dress children up like little adults, which looks odd, especially today. It's not uninteresting, but it had all been done so much that I thought, 'Okay, we're getting rid of all that, we're going to bring in color and range, get away from the leotards and tight pants, and get into something more generous for each character. Guy Caron and Guy Laliberté got right behind it. They could see that it would give the whole circus tradition a second wind."

Magie Continue, the 1986 show, would also be the first to feature an entirely original score, composed by René Dupéré. "I've always been attracted by world-beat music," Dupéré says, looking back. "My first attempt to incorporate it was in 1986. Nineteen eighty-six was a milestone because that was when we officially left street music behind and got into the modern/fusion/world-

"I THOUGHT THAT PERFORMERS SHOULD BE DRESSED IN A COORDINATED MANNER, FROM BEGINNING TO END, LIKE AT THE OPERA, OR IN A MUSICAL."

02/

01/
An artist performs
on the high wire, 1986.

02/
Increasingly, Cirque du Soleil began
to question and reinvent elements
of the circus tradition.

03/
Painting by artist Stéphane Jorisch,
inspired by Cirque du Soleil.

REINVENTING THE CIRCUS

If the 1986 show *Magie Continue* represented a step forward artistically, the show that toured North America in 1987 and 1989, *Le Cirque réinventé*, would represent an even bigger leap. While the company was still struggling financially, it had alleviated pressures enough to pour more resources into its next production. At the same time, changes occurred within the creative team that led to a bold new evolution in the creative process.

THE BIRTH OF A PROCESS

Until relatively recently, Cirque du Soleil shows haven't been written. Rather, they have emerged from a collaborative process between producer, creators, and individual artists. Beginning with *Le Cirque réinventé*, the costume designer began to invent characters for the show, sometimes adapted to a particular artist's idiosyncrasies. It was while developing such characters, and working out a theatrical approach, that Crête established a deep creative connection with Dragone.

"I started drawing characters for *Le Cirque réinventé*," Crête recalls. "At one point, I met Franco, who was directing the show, and I showed him my sketches. We really clicked."

"The chemistry between us was incredible," he adds. "His ideas for the mise-en-scène really jibed with mine. We were able to bounce ideas off one another, to provoke and stimulate each other. We still do."

PAINTING A SHOW

Under Dragone's guidance, the two worked out what might be called a "painterly" approach to show creation. "We really built the specific methodology that led to the creation of what we now recognize as Cirque du Soleil together," says Dragone. "I had been working with non-actors in Belgium, in the Théatre de Campus Company. For ten years, I had had to create shows with people who weren't used to creating shows. As a director, I had to learn how to let non-actors be expressive and right onstage. At the beginning of Cirque, we were all learning, nobody knew how to create a show without words that could touch people."

Dragone found his solution in the visual arts. "Very early in our history," he says, "I wanted to create, between the audience and the show, the same relation that exists between an individual and a painting. When you look at a painting, you don't know why you are moved and touched. I wanted to create images that could speak to the audience."

"For me," he says, specifying his role, "'director' is not a good word. Peter Brook is a big influence on my work. He says maybe the word 'distillator' is better."

Brook is an innovative British writer and director whose work in theater, film, and television has sometimes involved circus arts. Brook himself describes what the role of "distillator" is in his book *There Are No Secrets*. "We are aware that the conductor is not really making the music, it is making him," Brook writes. "If he is relaxed, open, and attuned, then the invisible will take possession of him; through him, it will reach us." In other words, Dragone, like Brook, believes that artists should be attuned to the possibilities of the reality around them, and should be a conduit between those possibilities and the audience.

One of the main reasons the creative team arrived at this approach was that a circus show must, by necessity, involve non-actors and a series of acrobatic acts. A painterly approach allowed the team to move away from a more formal structure to a more intuitive, freeform approach that is in its very essence difficult to quantify.

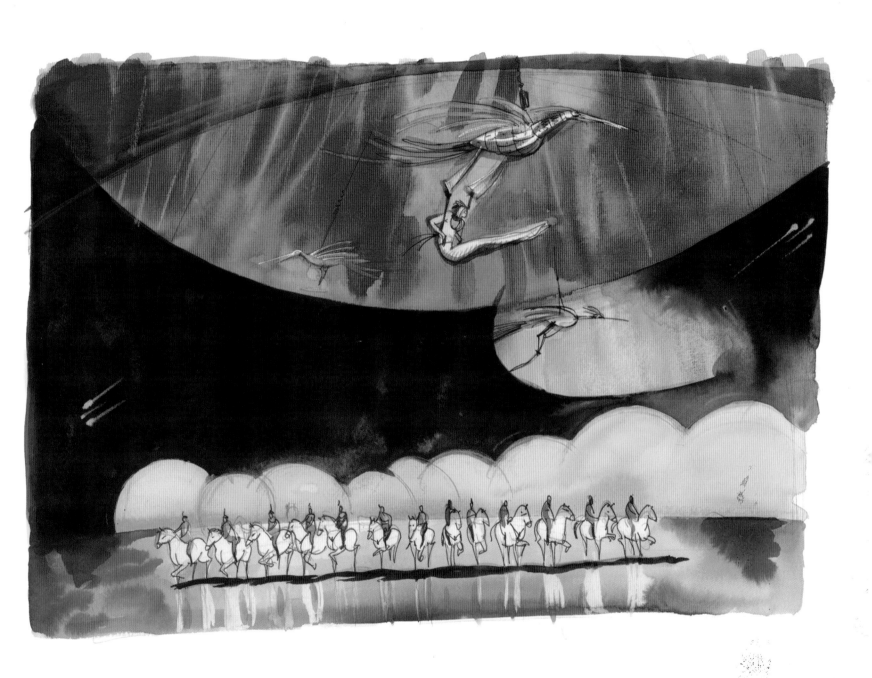

03/

SEARCHING FOR A UNIVERSAL LANGUAGE

The painterly approach also allowed Dragone and his team to achieve another goal: that of communicating in a language all audiences could understand. "When two babies come into the world, say in China and Belgium, they speak the same language," opines Dragone, "but then a process of socialization occurs, so they end up speaking and acting differently. And yet, despite the fact that each country has different social archetypes, there is a universal emotional archetype. We can cry in Belgium, or in China, or love in Belgium and in China for the same reasons. We wanted to create a language that was universal."

Appealing to the emotions allowed the creative team to embrace a freer form. Michel Crête explains: "We all came from the theater, and we were used to working with a script, and with directors who really wanted a good idea of what their set was going to be before they started doing anything else. That way, they could study the script in the context of the set design, and plan how to block the actors. All of this before rehearsals: that kind of rapid, detailed planning that leaves little room for happy accidents, for unexpected things to happen between performers."

"Our approach from the start was quite different," he continues. "We had no script. We started with a series of acrobatic performances that we knew had to be part of the show. There were very few certitudes to cling to going in. It's therefore very instinctive. Franco loves Peter Brook and he always started with what Brook calls a 'vague intuition.' You have to have a vague intuition about the show you're going to do."

In *There Are No Secrets* Brook himself describes the process of choosing a play's direction as essentially the result of unconscious, intuitive searching. He writes: "All the factors needed for a decision were already prepared in the unconscious part of the mind, without the conscious mind playing any part in the deliberations. This is why it is hard to answer the first question that is often asked—'How do you choose a play?' Is it accident or choice? Is it frivolous or the result of deep thoughts? Rather, I think, we prepare ourselves by the options we reject until the true solution, which was already there, suddenly comes into the open. One lives within a pattern: to ignore this is to take many false directions, but the moment the hidden movement is respected, it becomes the guide and in retrospect one can trace a clear pattern that continues to unfold."

Because the process is so unconscious and instinctual, it transcends language, and is difficult to describe. As far as the Dragone-era creative team is concerned, however, the best way to understand the process is the following.

"THERE IS A UNIVERSAL EMOTIONAL ARCHETYPE. WE CAN CRY IN BELGIUM, OR IN CHINA, OR LOVE IN BELGIUM AND IN CHINA FOR THE SAME REASONS. WE WANTED TO CREATE A LANGUAGE THAT WAS UNIVERSAL."

By exploring various thoughts and feelings freely, through reading, discussion, drawing, and free-form writing, the creators arrive at an organizing idea, or set of organizing ideas. This provides a hook onto which the rest of the creative process is loosely hung. In the case of *Le Cirque réinventé*, that hook came in the form of a character called the Monkey King.

"*Le Cirque réinventé* was inspired by a show by Cirque Grusse in Paris called *Paris-Peking*," remembers Caron. "It was about Marco Polo's voyages, and in the second part, Marco Polo meets the Monkey King. It was no good: there was no connection between the characters. The Monkey King didn't really fit. But there was a commedia dell'arte element that I thought we should incorporate. At the National Circus School, I had a student called Marc Proulx, who was good at commedia dell'arte and kung fu, and he was absorbed by everything Chinese. And I thought, 'This is the man! This is the King of Fools!' I showed the character to Franco, and he said, 'My God! We've got it!'"

Perhaps one of the most surprising things about Cirque du Soleil's explosive development over twenty years is the almost provisional nature of its creative process, based as it has been on intuition. Yet it was by embracing happy accidents that Cirque was able to blossom creatively. Composer René Dupéré puts it this way: "People might think that we set out to reinvent the circus, and then just did it. But things don't happen that way. We were just a bunch of crazy people who wanted to do things, and little by little we came to a vision of what the modern circus could be." He continues: "I wrote four shows before the 1987 show happened. It took four years before we arrived at a more mature show, a more united series of acts linked together by music. It's not something we decided to do, like that. There were a lot of coincidences along the way, and we just went with it. There is no recipe, that's for sure."

At the heart of the creative team, there was never any doubt that success would be achieved. "I was sure and absolutely convinced that the shows would succeed," claims Franco Dragone today. "Sometimes we disagreed, but Guy Laliberté always trusted what I was doing."

GUY LALIBERTÉ AS CREATOR

Some producers—even creative producers like Guy Laliberté—might naturally be terrified by a process as uncertain as that developed by his creative team early on, especially in light of growing financial pressure. Laliberté has not only embraced and supported it, but has been an active participant from the beginning.

"I was always close to the creators, having been one myself," he says. "I knew what the creative process was all about. I got to choose people I had confidence in, and I gave them a clear path, without obstacles. Since I had confidence in them, I knew I was making a good decision."

"I said, 'I believe in the idea of a work-in-progress, I believe we'll get where we want to go,'" he continues. "I did it knowing I had a certain amount of security, because we built each of our shows around good acts, what I call the 'acrobatic skeleton.' So I told myself that, if we make mistakes with the mise-en-scène, or on the artistic level, well, we've got good acts, and at least that's something. I knew that, at the level of the acts alone, we could compete with any circus."

Gilles Ste-Croix describes Laliberté's involvement in a show as "very creative." "He contributes ten percent," specifies Ste-Croix. "He gives the first five percent and the last five percent. And that ten percent makes a difference as to whether the show is a success or not. The first five percent is that he'll approve the creative team, the acrobatic skeleton, and a general direction to go in. He travels all over the world, so he has a great idea of what audiences are expecting."

"The last five percent," he continues, "is that he knows when a show is good or not, instinctively. He'll say, 'The rhythm is not right.' He follows up as things go along."

Laliberté agrees with Ste-Croix's assessment. "That's why, when we talked about what to call me in the program, we decided on 'Guide.' I'm a creative producer, not just a business producer." After having been involved with setting the course of a show, he gives the creative team free rein, checking in occasionally. He will normally become involved again as it nears its premiere. "It's mainly to give fresh eyes to the process," he explains. "I can be more objective, because I haven't been involved day to day. Sometimes I can see that there were objectives we had at the beginning that we've strayed from. I think I have a good sense of showmanship, so I'll always have a word to say about that. If the show's become too poetic, I'll say it."

Laliberté is not afraid to perform last-minute, radical surgery if he feels a show does not live up to his expectations. A typical example occurred during the production of *La Nouba*, in late 1998. Days away from the premiere, Laliberté watched a rehearsal and decided that the show was not dynamic enough. To fix it, he insisted that an acrobatic cycling act be added. The eleventh-hour addition threw the entire timing and structure of the show off, leaving the creators and cast very little time to adjust. Nevertheless, adjust they did, and the show continues to win audiences over today.

Given his background in folk music, it's not surprising that Laliberté also takes a particular interest in music. "Music is one of my passions," he says fondly, "so I have a lot to say there, too."

"I KNEW WHAT THE CREATIVE PROCESS WAS ALL ABOUT. I GOT TO CHOOSE PEOPLE I HAD CONFIDENCE IN, AND I GAVE THEM A CLEAR PATH, WITHOUT OBSTACLES. SINCE I HAD CONFIDENCE IN THEM, I KNEW I WAS MAKING A GOOD DECISION."

05/

Los Angeles Festival

© 1985 L.A. Festival ®

06/

WINNING THE L.A. GAMBLE

With *Le Cirque réinventé*, Cirque du Soleil delivered a winner. The new approach to theatricality and circus blew audiences away.

Cirque knew it had a great show on its hands. But was *Le Cirque réinventé* special enough to bet the company's entire future on? That was the question Cirque du Soleil had to face head-on when it was given a once-in-a-lifetime opportunity to perform for the most important audience of its career, at the Los Angeles Festival in 1987. To answer the call meant gambling everything Cirque had earned so far. If the L.A. audience failed to respond, its career would be stopped dead in its tracks.

The story of the 1987 Los Angeles Festival marks the first turning point in the history of Cirque du Soleil.

"YOU CLIMBED INSIDE THIS YELLOW AND BLUE TENT, AND IT EXPLODED OUT. IT WAS AS IF IT WAS BIGGER THAN ANYTHING THE TENT COULD CONTAIN."

OPPORTUNITY KNOCKS

Cirque's first opportunity to play Los Angeles, in September 1987, came from the Quebec government. In the documentary film *Run Before You Fly*, Thomas Schumacher, who was head of the Los Angeles Festival at the time, remembers: "I get a lot of credit for saying that I saw Cirque du Soleil and told them to come to the Los Angeles Festival. It actually happened through a man at the Quebec Delegation called Michel Robitaille."

Schumacher continues: "I went to have lunch with him one day to say, 'I want money to bring Montreal dancer and choreographer Edouard Locke to L.A., to the Festival.' I needed $50,000 to cover travel or something. And he said, 'We'll give you funding to bring Edouard Locke and La La La Human Steps, but I want you to go see a circus.' I laughed at him and said, 'We're not going to bring a circus to the L.A. Festival. It's an arts festival!'"

Seeing Cirque du Soleil on videotape changed Schumacher's mind. "It was a Wednesday," he recalls. "I went back to his office,

I watched a videotape. I was blown away, and Friday night I was in Quebec City. Guy Laliberté picked me up at the airport and drove me to the site. I saw the second half of the show that night. I saw it twice Saturday, twice on Sunday, and we made the decision Sunday night."

Schumacher describes the effect *Le Cirque réinventé* had on him in glowing terms. "What we saw was what everyone in Montreal and in Quebec had been seeing for years, which was complete magic because you climbed inside this yellow and blue tent, and it exploded out. It was as if it was bigger than anything the tent could contain.

LET'S MAKE A DEAL

Though Schumacher wanted Cirque du Soleil for his festival, he couldn't afford to pay them. "A lot of people don't realize that, when we brought Cirque to America, by the time we booked it, it would have been way too expensive to spend the festival's money to bring them," he says.

Despite this, Laliberté says the opportunity was too good to pass up: "I thought, 'I'm not going to wait twenty years to see if we can make a living off what we do. The opportunity is here, let's make a deal. I told Thomas Schumacher, 'Give us the opening slot, promotion, and one hundred percent of the gate.'"

"TO LIVE OR DIE IN L.A."

Laliberté habitually refers to the Los Angeles Festival gambit as Cirque's "to live or die in L.A." moment. The simple truth is, at that particular moment in Cirque du Soleil's history, it could only afford a one-way trip to Los Angeles. Transporting the cast, crew, and equipment across the continent from Montreal to Los Angeles stretched Cirque's finances to the very limit. If they didn't earn enough money at the gate, Cirque could not afford to return home. Cirque du Soleil's story would end there.

FLAVOR OF THE MONTH

It didn't, of course. The gamble paid off, big time. Simply put, Cirque du Soleil was a smash in Los Angeles; in Laliberté's words, "the flavor of the month." The deal worked out beautifully for Cirque. "Thomas Schumacher always says it was the worst deal he ever made in the history of the festival," Guy Laliberté says, smiling. "He thought he was saving money, but he could have made a bundle if he'd kept part of the gate."

Celebrities and entertainment executives flocked to the show, which led to producers, says Laliberté, "coming to us and offering us the world." Faced with temptation, Cirque kept its feet on the ground. "We almost made a deal with Columbia Pictures, who wanted to do a film about the history of Cirque," remembers Laliberté. "But at the last minute, we realized that they were actually trying to buy us lock, stock, and barrel, so we pulled out. They wanted all the rights."

A relationship with the Walt Disney Corporation that started in L.A. in 1987 eventually did result in a partnership. In *Run Before You Fly*, Disney's Michael Eisner recalls: "From the moment I saw it to the moment I was able to make an arrangement with Guy Laliberté, I was obsessed by Cirque du Soleil, obsessed to get it as part of the Disney entertainment complex. I tried to interest them in being acquired by Disney, and they weren't interested in that. And, boy, were they right!"

By the end of 1987, Cirque du Soleil was out of debt. After a successful run in Santa Monica, *Le Cirque réinventé* played New York City in 1988. "We ended up in a great financial situation for a young company by the end of 1988, with a couple million dollars' profit," says Laliberté.

Unfortunately, that success would be undercut by an internal crisis in the following year.

"IF THEY DIDN'T EARN ENOUGH MONEY AT THE GATE, CIRQUE COULD NOT AFFORD TO RETURN HOME. CIRQUE DU SOLEIL'S STORY WOULD END THERE."

FIRST GROWING PAINS

From the vantage point of the creative team, things couldn't have been better at the end of 1988. Franco Dragone recalls: "I was in New York, with a journalist who didn't particularly like Cirque, and I told her that, in a few years, this circus would be known around the world. I was sure about it."

In the middle of its new success, however, Cirque du Soleil was rocked when Guy Caron left the company, taking a number of others with him.

A FAMILY SQUABBLE

At the root of Caron's decision, according to Laliberté, was a fundamental disagreement about the company's business orientation. "At the artistic level," Laliberté explains, "we were always on the same wavelength. Caron and I had the same goal: creating a circus in Quebec. But we had a difference of opinion about how to make it happen in 1987, and that led to him leaving in 1988."

Part of the disagreement had to do with Cirque du Soleil's relationship with the National Circus School. "Caron saw a symbiosis between the Circus School and Cirque," Laliberté elaborates. "He thought they should grow together. But I said, 'No, it's a business.' That led to conflict."

"When we became a success in the U.S.," he continues, "I thought we should put a second show on the road, with a new set of artists. Guy Caron thought the money should go back into a pot, with some of it going back to the school, and I said, 'No, we're going to create a circus that's going to be its own thing.' So Caron left, and the Circus School remained independent."

Laliberté believes that, at its root, the rupture between him and Caron can be traced back to Cirque's origins in cooperatives and communes. "You have to remember that we started as a nonprofit organization. And Guy Caron was into cooperatives, the collective. He was institutionally minded, and I had a business goal."

Today, he defends his point of view. "I always had business goals, as much as I had goals to travel and have fun. You can't help it when you're in your early twenties, like I was, and you're handling a $1.6 million budget. We had a responsibility to the people who gave us a contract, and I had a long-term goal, too. I wanted to keep this going. There was a planet to discover, and it was clear that there was an opportunity, not only to do something creative, but also to succeed as a business. I always said that if Cirque makes it big, it will be because it succeeds at marrying art and business."

Unfortunately, a number of artists loyal to Caron decided to leave with him, leaving Laliberté with the challenge of making up for the loss. According to Laliberté, some of the artists had become upset at his plans for the future. "We had decided to start work on another show, called *Eclipse,* with a new tent design, something even more revolutionary. I wanted to keep *Le Cirque réinventé* on the road with the original artists while we brought in new artists to work on the second show. That upset a lot of people on *Le Cirque réinventé*, because they wanted to be part of a new show, too. They saw themselves as pioneers with the first show, and they believed that gave them an automatic right to be in the second show. That's what they expected. That caused a lot of tension."

Because of the tensions, plans for *Eclipse* had to be shelved, and development costs for the show absorbed.

GILLES STE-CROIX TAKES OVER

To replace Caron and help put Cirque back on track with new artists, Laliberté appointed his old friend Gilles Ste-Croix as artistic director.

When he returned to Cirque after a nearly four-year hiatus, Ste-Croix realized that his first job would be to earn the trust of the Caron loyalists who had stayed behind. "They saw me as Guy Laliberté's man," Ste-Croix explains.

Additional problems presented themselves in the form of Normand Latourelle, an old acquaintance who had become a partner in the company. "We had known Normand as far back as 1984," remembers Laliberté. "He had been in charge of some of the 450th anniversary celebration programming in Québec City, and we shared an office. By 1986, we had hired him as Assistant General Manager, but he left at the end of the year, for a couple of reasons. He wanted to be General Manager, and I wasn't ready for that. He didn't think we should take the gamble and go to L.A. I was convinced that we should, because I knew that our potential for growth lay in succeeding in a big way in the States. Latourelle thought we should go slow, maybe try a small American border market, like Plattsburgh, first. So he left."

"That's when I made another mistake," continues Laliberté, "because, when he left, I asked him to find his replacement. And the guy he found to take his place was a disaster. So by six months later, Daniel Gauthier was completely overloaded. Daniel came to me with an ultimatum: 'If Normand doesn't come back, I'm leaving.'"

Latourelle would only return to Cirque du Soleil under two conditions. One was that he become General Manager. The second was that he become a full partner with Gauthier and Laliberté in Cirque du Soleil, which was in the process of being transformed from a nonprofit corporation to a for-profit company.* "I always said that I'd be happier being one-third partner in something that was worth a million dollars than being the only owner of a company worth ten dollars," says Laliberté, "so I said 'yes'. We had an agreement: Daniel would take care of Finance and Administration, Normand would handle Marketing and Operations, and I would be in charge of Business Development and

07/
A Cirque performance explodes with colour. At times in its history, as many risks were taken offstage as on.

08/
Character design by Dominique Lemieux. West Coast audiences in the U.S. were hooked by the pageantry and imagination of the new circus from Québec.

10/
Gilles Ste-Croix brings new meaning to the term "street performer," 1982.

11/
Cirque du Soleil raises the Grand Chapiteau for the first time in London, England.

Creation. I thought that splitting the responsibility this way would leave me free to build on the success we had in Los Angeles."

By 1989, however, Latourelle had begun to engineer a putsch against Laliberté. "He actually helped to exacerbate the problem we were having with the artists at the time," Laliberté remembers. "He had made financial promises to the artists that Daniel and I were never aware of, you know: 'Just hold on, we'll make things better for you, don't worry'... In fact, he had promised them the money that we wanted to put into *Eclipse*, and, of course, he couldn't deliver on it. That added to the tension and disappointment they felt when we tried to get *Eclipse* off the ground. The worst thing is, he was talking out of both sides of his mouth. Gilles always remembers being in a meeting where Latourelle said: 'Artists are always more creative when they're starving.' Gilles thought: 'You've never been an artist if you say that, man.' I can say truthfully that I've always tried to improve working conditions for artists. I'm not sure Latourelle can."

The tension between Latourelle and Laliberté continued for months. Eventually, Latourelle convinced Daniel Gauthier that Laliberté should be pushed aside, and accept reduced creative responsibility. At the same time, he was asked to relinquish any responsibility over company operations. In essence, Latourelle was acting against the initial partnership agreement between himself, Gauthier, and Laliberté. "I come from the street, where you take partnerships seriously," says Laliberté. "You say, 'I watch your back, you watch mine.' So I take it very personally when I feel someone is betraying an agreement." When presented with the ultimatum, Laliberté responded with one of his own. "I bluffed: I told Daniel, 'It's either him or me,'" remembers Laliberté, "and I acted on the bluff. I didn't show up to work for three days. That convinced Daniel I was serious."

Latourelle was bought out, and Gauthier became Laliberté's only partner in Cirque du Soleil. "Latourelle really didn't believe we were going to make it," says Laliberté. "I remember he told Dany Pelchat (who eventually became General Manager): 'Just make sure the company stays afloat long enough for me to cash my last check.' Looking back, I believe that Daniel really thought it through, and came to the right decision as far as Cirque's fu-

ture. I'm very grateful to him for that. I think he recognized what was best for Cirque du Soleil."

"As for Normand, I think he was a great marketer, and great at selling tickets. But his management style, and his way of working with people, just didn't fit the culture of Cirque du Soleil as I see it. He didn't share the company vision: a vision based on trust, respect, and open-mindedness."

Dealing with internal tension hurt the company. Having made money in 1987, Cirque ended up in a deficit situation once again in 1989. They also went back to the West Coast, with less-than-spectacular results. "We tried to revamp *Le Cirque réinventé* and bring it to Los Angeles," remembers Laliberté. "We brought in a new director, Michel Barette. But the reaction wasn't great. People said, 'This is just warmed over.' It became obvious that we had to do something totally new."

That "something" was a show called *Nouvelle Expérience*. It would incorporate the best ideas from the aborted *Eclipse* project, and would revolutionize the circus arts. Following the show's premiere in 1990, Cirque du Soleil would be propelled on an upward course that continues to this day.

* In 1987, Cirque du Soleil became a private company, after having been a nonprofit organization since 1984. "From the beginning," says Laliberté, "that was our goal. I told the government funding agencies that we'd be free of needing their support within five years. At one point in those five years, we actually returned a subsidy check that we had received, because we'd made money." Members of the nonprofit company agreed to give up their interest in exchange for permanent employment.

10/

CIRQUE DU SOLEIL'S
FIRST EUROPEAN VENTURE

IN 1990, **LE CIRQUE RÉINVENTÉ** PLAYED IN PARIS AND LONDON FOR THE FIRST TIME. THE EXPERIENCE HELPED THEM TO GAIN A BETTER UNDERSTANDING OF HOW AUDIENCE EXPECTATIONS CAN DIFFER FROM COUNTRY TO COUNTRY. IN THE END, THE BRIEF EUROPEAN TOUR PROVIDED A VALUABLE LESSON IN HOW TO BECOME A TRULY INTERNATIONAL ENTERTAINER.

Sylvie Galarneau was assistant stage manager at the time. "The reaction of European audiences was not good," she says now. "The way we evaluated audience response back then was by comparing it to the reaction we got on the West Coast, where we had our biggest audiences, our biggest fans. But London was rough. It was summer, so most of the British people were out of the city. It was mostly foreigners who didn't know us, or didn't want to see a circus that much, because they were traveling to London to see the attractions there. We had lousy reviews, we didn't sell many tickets."

Laliberté adds that London was in the middle of a heat wave, "so even people who bought tickets wouldn't come, because it was so hot."

Galarneau remembers her experience in Paris a little more fondly. "We moved to Paris," she says, "at Le Cirque d'Hiver. We did pretty well there, for our first time in Paris. But it was fall, and, at one point, there were sixteen circuses in town at the same time. And the cost of being in Europe was an unexpected surprise. So, shortly before Christmas, they said: 'Okay, we've made our entry into Europe, it's time to go.'"

Nicholas Dewhurst, who, like his father Brian, is from a circus family, performed in the show. He puts the period in perspective: "The show wasn't a success. It closed in Paris. I think part of the reason was that the show was called *Le Cirque réinventé*, but, in Europe, that wasn't true. A lot of alternative circuses had already done that. It was nothing new to audiences in London and Paris. They'd seen it all before. So it got a bad rap."

Guy Laliberté puts a more positive spin on the experience. "We made money in Paris," he asserts. "People think we didn't, but we did. We weren't successful with the critics or the press. We had difficulties, but we made money."

"The reason we didn't keep going," he makes clear, "was the Gulf War. Everything was a panic in Europe. There was a lot of political and social uncertainty, so we made a business decision. We thought: 'We're too fragile to go ahead in this climate.' We didn't have our own tent, our own means . . . we were compromised." Once again, Cirque made a decision to do things its own way: "We decided that, when we came back, we'd be back as one hundred percent Cirque du Soleil, all the way, no compromise."

PART 2

CREATING WORLDS UPON WORLDS

CIRQUE DU SOLEIL'S GROWTH THROUGHOUT THE 1990s WAS EXPLOSIVE. CIRQUE WENT FROM A SINGLE SHOW TOURING NORTH AMERICA TO FOUR SHOWS ON TOUR SIMULTANEOUSLY AROUND THE WORLD. BY 1999, IT ALSO HAD THREE SUCCESSFUL RESIDENT SHOWS RUNNING, TWO OF WHICH HAVE BREATHED NEW LIFE INTO LAS VEGAS ENTERTAINMENT. IN GUY LALIBERTÉ'S UNDERSTATED WORDS, THE COMPANY GREW FROM A "SMALL BUSINESS" INTO "A SMALL MULTINATIONAL."

IN A WAY, THE HISTORY OF CIRQUE DU SOLEIL CEASED TO BE "HISTORY" AT ALL WITH THE PREMIERE OF **SALTIMBANCO** IN 1992. IN CIRQUE'S TWENTIETH YEAR, ALL OF ITS SHOWS FROM **SALTIMBANCO** ON ARE STILL PLAYING, CONSTANTLY BEING REINVENTED AND RETOOLED FOR NEW AUDIENCES. STILL FRESH AND RELEVANT, THESE SHOWS ARE FEATURES OF THE PRESENT, NOT RELICS OF THE PAST.

CHAPTER
7

NOUVELLE EXPÉRIENCE
REINVENTING THE CIRCUS AGAIN

> CIRQUE DU SOLEIL BACKED ITS 1990 SHOW WITH ITS BIGGEST BUDGET YET. "IT WAS A BIG, BIG SHOW FOR US," REMEMBERS GUY LALIBERTÉ. "WE REALLY SHOWED WHAT WE COULD DO WITH MONEY. WE GOT A BIGGER TENT (2,500 SEATS), A NEW SET, MORE REFINED COSTUMES. WE HAD THE REAL GOODS."

A NEW ALCHEMY

Once again, Franco Dragone was asked to direct the show. This time, according to Gilles Ste-Croix, he was reluctant to return. "Franco would only commit if certain changes were made. He said, 'If I'm going to work with you again, I want to build a cohesive team.'"

Dominique Lemieux, who had worked briefly on *Le Cirque réinventé*, was called in to replace Michel Crête as costume designer. Crête became set designer. Together, Lemieux, Crête, and Dragone established a creative rapport that would have an enormous impact on Cirque.

Crête was more than pleased to have someone else look after costumes. "After I'm done on a project, I like to move on," he says. "Except that, as costume designer on *Le Cirque réinventé*, I couldn't. A month after the premiere, new artists came onboard, and they needed costumes, too. There was always some kind of follow-up involved. I really wasn't into it.

So I asked Dominique Lemieux if she would take over for me. Like me, she really clicked with Franco."

Recalling her first encounters with Dragone, Lemieux says: "I found the way Franco worked, so closely and directly with the artists, fantastic. He'd say one word and get results. He barely had to talk to me, and images would come into my head. It was a real meeting of the minds."

MINING "VAGUE INTUITION"

This new creative cohesion allowed Cirque to plunge even more deeply into the creative process it had established in previous shows. "During the creation of *Nouvelle Expérience*," Gilles Ste-Croix recalls, "we started to say, 'What are we going to talk about?' And Michel would say, 'Well, what are we concerned about?' We said, 'Life in the circus, globalization.' We'd get books, magazines, and we'd create a common treasure, which was fuel to all the creators."

Ste-Croix goes on to describe the team's creative process. Referring to the shows made with Dragone as director in the 1990s, he says: "There's Guy's wish list, Franco's ideas, and then Michel will see what's pertinent. Dominique will create images from Franco's fantasies. She'll draw five hundred characters, and Franco will use sixty. Or, out of the drawings, he'll say, 'See this arm here, make another character from that.' And she draws very automatically. She's always amazed at what comes out."

"We always start from an idea," says Lemieux, describing the process from her perspective. "It will evolve as we work through it. When we've got something that seems to make sense, we go home, and I start drawing characters. Michel will draw sets, and Franco will keep doing research. It's just a point of departure. It doesn't mean we'll stick with it throughout the work."

The high level of collaboration will extend beyond the core creative team to other key members of the team. Long-time Cirque contributors like choreographer Debra Brown and lighting designer Luc Lafortune are asked to contribute thoughts and ideas from the earliest stages of the creative process.

For *Nouvelle Expérience*, that basic idea came from a novel by the nineteenth century science-fiction novelist Jules Verne.

"*Nouvelle Expérience*," says Franco Dragone, "was inspired by a book by Jules Verne called *La Chasse au Météore*, about this meteorite made of gold that was going to hit the earth, which meant that everybody would try to find where it fell. I took that idea, and told myself that, if a meteorite was going to hit the earth, it would break into a thousand pieces, and each piece would be a little jewel somewhere. Our show would be a trip across the planet to find these little jewels." For Dragone, *Nouvelle Expérience* would mirror a voyage of discovery that Cirque du Soleil itself was on. "The acts and characters were jewels found all over the planet."

The idea of a journey around the world intrinsically dovetailed with the creative team's feelings about the state of the global environment. "The idea that the earth was Gaia, a living being we had to respect, was big at the time," explains Dragone. "The planet is not this inert thing. If the human race is going to continue, we have to respect that, and preserve the planet's riches."

"NOUVELLE EXPÉRIENCE WOULD MIRROR A VOYAGE OF DISCOVERY THAT CIRQUE DU SOLEIL ITSELF WAS ON. THE ACTS AND CHARACTERS WERE JEWELS FOUND ALL OVER THE PLANET."

FRONTISPIECE/
CIRQUE DU SOLEIL'S GRAND CHAPITEAU
IN TORONTO, EARLY 1990.

01/
BRIAN DEWHURST AS THE GREAT
CHAMBERLAIN.

02/
NOUVELLE EXPÉRIENCE'S MADAME
CORPORATION.

02/

YOU ARE THE AUTHOR

For Michel Crête, the creative process Cirque began to explore with *Nouvelle Expérience* is not limited to the creative team. The audience is part of the process, too. By working as freely and openly as it does, Cirque creates space for people's imagination to fill. "We create words or images that are provoking and stimulating enough for each spectator, according to his or her background, history, and culture, to invent a personal world that complements the show," he explains.

Crête adds that, in the final analysis, the spectator's contribution may be more important than the creators'. "I'm not sure how important the concepts we organized our shows around are to the spectator," he says. "They were important to us as creators,

because they allowed us to build the shows around them. But it really doesn't matter if the audience has any access to our thoughts and ideas. We would have press conferences in which we'd describe our process, and people would go to the show looking for things. But that's crazy."

"The audience shouldn't be forced to look for our motivations," he continues. "Audience members should show up with their own personal backgrounds and get what they want out of the show." Quoting the late Francis Bacon, regarded as Britain's most important twentieth-century painter, Crête says: "'The minute you tell a story with a painting, the painting becomes boring, because the story becomes more powerful than the painting.'"

"AUDIENCE MEMBERS SHOULD SHOW UP WITH THEIR OWN PERSONAL BACKGROUNDS AND GET WHAT THEY WANT OUT OF THE SHOW."

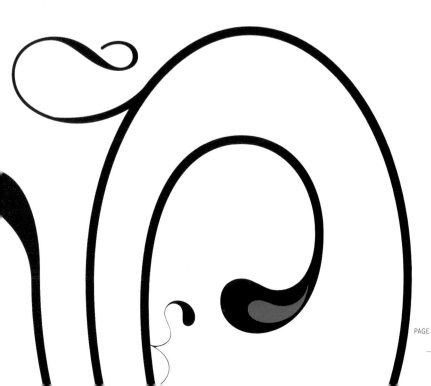

TRUSTING THE PROCESS

As he had from the beginning of Cirque, Laliberté oversaw the creative process. He backed his creative team's risk-taking every step of the way. Dominique Lemieux remembers his characteristic sangfroid: "Guy always had an opinion about the music and the acrobatic skeleton. Aside from that, he had a lot of confidence in us. He'd tell us very frankly what he thought, and sometimes we wouldn't agree, but he had enormous confidence in us. I found him extraordinary, because he was under tremendous pressure."

04/

03/
LIFANG WANG, FOOT JUGGLING.

04/
THE NEW LOOK: CIRQUE DU SOLEIL, IN
COSTUMES DESIGNED BY DOMINIQUE
LEMIEUX, TAKES THE STAGE.

05/
THE DEVILS.

05/

INNOVATIONS IN SET DESIGN

Nouvelle Expérience represented a bold new direction in terms of set design. Michel Crête's ideas turned the Grand Chapiteau into a rich experience of theater-in-the-round.

"We started to question the whole physical setup inside a big top," Crête explains. "We had been working with a circular ring, like people used to do in the nineteenth century. Except that, back then, the ring had been designed like that so horses had a place to run around in. So why not create a theatrical space, instead? We also got rid of the arch through which the performers and animals used to come and go. There was a fabulous space reserved for backstage, to separate the public from the performers with these huge velour curtains. So we got rid of all that, and, for the first time in a circus show, the public had access to all of this circular space within the big top."

For Crête, the decision had an immediate impact on the performing artists, pushing them even deeper into theatrical expression. "The idea was to make the artists consciously aware, as they were leaving the artists' tent and coming into the corridor that led into the big top, that they were becoming part of a show," he says.

"For instance, in the traditional circus," Crête continues, "when an artist finished his performance, he just disappeared backstage, out of the scene. But with all the old structures gone, the artist couldn't just disappear. He or she was still onstage, going somewhere. But where? The notion of a space that became a set, a whole other universe, opened up the show for us. It also gives each character in the show more power, because they have a space to inhabit, and an arc to follow within that space."

Previous Cirque shows had deliberately blurred the line between audience and performer, drawing the audience more deeply into the show. Crête's innovation in set design would erase it even further. "When you have a central performance area in the middle of a big top, with spectators all around, there's a feeling that everyone is in the same space, performers and audience alike," he explains. "There's no 'fourth wall' between them, like in a traditional theater."

06/

06/
LIFANG WANG PERFORMS
FOOT JUGGLING.

07/
NOUVELLE EXPÉRIENCE'S DEVILS.

07/

A MORE ELABORATE MUSICAL LANGUAGE

Composer René Dupéré also saw *Nouvelle Expérience* as an opportunity to push his ideas further. Cirque shows had already been sung in an invented language. In the new show, Dupéré extended its possibilities.

"We really wanted the music to be an actor in itself, to be the speech of the show, the narration of the show," Dupéré says. Describing the origin of "Cirque language," Dupéré says, "I actually used African phonemes when writing some of the 'words' to the music. I got them from a friend of mine who wrote lullabies, from Rwanda. I just mixed them together and made rhymes, so it would sound like poetry. There's a structure to it, but there's no meaning."

TURNING ATHLETES INTO ARTISTS

With *Nouvelle Expérience*, Dragone was given the time he needed to explore his work with performers more deeply. In extensive workshopping sessions involving experiments with movement and role-playing, Franco pulled each performer to a higher level of artistic expression.

For Guy Laliberté, pushing the artists in this direction made sense for the ultimate success of *Nouvelle Expérience*, and all future Cirque du Soleil productions. "Each show plays between 385 and 490 times a year," he explains, "and that means artists going out and giving one hundred and fifty percent each show to make the public happy. They've got the tough job at Cirque. The creators have it easy: once the show is up and running, it's in the artists' hands."

"We always believed that what will keep the artists committed and stop them from getting bored is making sure the shows change and evolve, and that they can grow with it," adds Laliberté. "I'm sure it works when I see shows of ours that have been on the road for ten years—you can see the light in the performers' eyes, and the effect it has on the audience."

Curiously, this new dedication came at a time when Cirque du Soleil began to hire an increasing number of high-performance gymnasts as performers. The opportunity was too strong for Laliberté, ever mindful of his "acrobatic skeleton," to resist. "We knew what high caliber was," he says, "and we had a great program starting in 1987, especially in light of our means at the time. But in 1990, we *really* came in with top-quality acts."

08/

"WE REALLY WANTED THE MUSIC TO BE AN ACTOR IN ITSELF, TO BE THE SPEECH OF THE SHOW, THE NARRATION OF THE SHOW."

08/
A PARADE OF MUSICAL CHARACTERS FOR
NOUVELLE EXPÉRIENCE, SKETCHED BY
DOMINIQUE LEMIEUX.

A PROCESS IN CLOSE-UP

Franco's workshopping methods with artists became the rule at Cirque du Soleil from *Nouvelle Expérience* onward. The ultimate goal has been for the artists to arrive at a truer, more complete expression of their inner selves. During the workshopping process, the costume designer seeks inspiration for characters from the artists' personalities. During the life of a show, the artist will then constantly seek to make his or her character evolve.

For athletes—who have come from a world as far removed from Dragone's methods as one can imagine—the experience has proven to be both challenging and rewarding.

Michael Rosenberger, a national-level gymnast who has performed in three Cirque shows, gives a fairly typical appraisal of the process. "To do those workshops was completely different and challenging," he says. "It was fun, but it could also be draining. Some days were really long, and you'd be there really late, and sometimes you never knew what they wanted."

Because Dragone's approach relies so much on intuition and experimentation, the sessions could be daunting. "Franco would ask you to propose something," says Rosenberger, "but you would never be sure what he wanted. You'd try something, and it wouldn't work. And then you'd do something and he would say, 'Yes!' It was stressful. You're trying to do something creative, you're trying to please this person, and you don't always know what to do."

Many of the gymnasts interviewed for this book describe the workshopping sessions as mentally confusing and physically demanding. Simon Tinhan, an artist in *Mystère*, remembers: "I was in Montreal five, six months for training. I had to learn dance, some acting, comedy. Sometimes I liked it, other times I'd say: 'What for? Why do I need to do this?' Like the time they said: 'Move like a snake, like a frog.'"

Other artists remember instructions like "be Monday," "be Tuesday," "be a tomato," "be rain," or "be a butterfly" (this last came with the added recollection: "That was easier, at least a butterfly *moves*").

Danielle Rodenkirchen, a national gymnast for Canada before joining the cast of *Alegría*, says: "Some things were just testing our limits, like we'd have to strike these poses and keep them for hours on end. I remember one in particular: we had to arch our backs all the way and keep our mouths open, and we were there for an hour until he called on us."

Konstantin Besstchetnyi, who performs in *Quidam*, describes feeling particularly exposed. "Working with Franco was strange," he recalls. "He asked us to take off our clothes and we were almost naked, just underwear. He made us walk around in a circle for half an hour."

These challenges were particularly trying for gymnasts, who come from a culture where experimentation is entirely frowned upon. Paul Bowler, an Olympic competitor who now performs in *Mystère*, sums up the differences this way: "When you do gymnastics, there's a book that says, 'You need to do a crucifix, a handstand, a double-back somersault, etc. to get 10.' Six men will judge you and they're going to copy down every mistake you make, then they'll blast it and show 15,000 people how not-perfect you are. That's gymnastics in a nutshell."

FOR ATHLETES—WHO HAVE COME FROM A WORLD AS FAR REMOVED FROM DRAGONE'S METHODS AS ONE CAN IMAGINE—THE EXPERIENCE HAS PROVEN TO BE BOTH CHALLENGING AND REWARDING.

10/

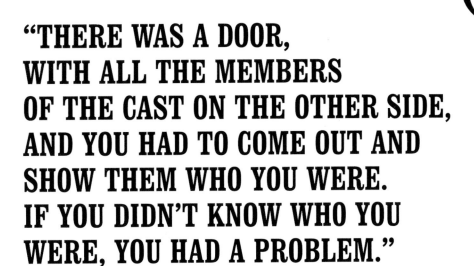

"THERE WAS A DOOR, WITH ALL THE MEMBERS OF THE CAST ON THE OTHER SIDE, AND YOU HAD TO COME OUT AND SHOW THEM WHO YOU WERE. IF YOU DIDN'T KNOW WHO YOU WERE, YOU HAD A PROBLEM."

For female competitors, the strictness of the high-level gymnastics regimen can be even more paralyzing. Natasha Hallett, another performer in *Mystère*, comments: "I didn't want to stay in gymnastics. My coach was abusive. We weren't allowed to eat, to smile in the gym, to have fun, to listen to music. Everything was 'no, no, no.'... A lot of people go crazy after gymnastics, because they're restricted from doing so much at such a young age. With Cirque, I went from this completely restrictive environment to complete freedom."

Ultimately, the artists realize that the workshop exercises are part of a larger strategy. "I realize now," says Rodenkirchen, "that Franco was breaking us down and seeing what he could use." Besstchetnyi adds: "He knows how to find the strong part in everybody." With this realization often comes acceptance, and release.

For some, like Terry Bartlett—a three-time Olympic competitor for the United Kingdom who now performs in "O"—the transition occurs almost immediately. "When I auditioned for Franco," Bartlett remembers, "he said things like: 'Jump with happiness.' And I thought: 'I think I get this.' I absolutely loved it." For others, the transition to joy and self-realization is slower but no less real. Looking back, Natasha Hallett says of the process:

"I loved it. It was like discovering things about myself I had no idea were there. That transition . . . you learn so much about yourself, and your talents in other areas. You go, 'Yeah, I can be funny, I can express myself.' The hardest part of the training process was 'The Door.' There was a door, with all the members of the cast on the other side, and you had to come out and show them who you were. If you didn't know who you were, you had a problem. That was really what he was trying to get at. What is it inside you that makes you special? I think that's what Cirque brought to an extreme."

Nathalie Bollinger, who performs in "O", traces the full arc of the process. "The workshop with Franco was fantastic. He's an amazing person, he really gets everything out of you. A friend of mine was in *Nouvelle Expérience*, and she said: 'Cirque will change you, no matter what you think.' I said: 'Okay, whatever.' But it does, it allows you the freedom you wouldn't get anywhere else. I think that, in normal life, you may be narrow-minded, because society doesn't let you go out of bounds. But in Cirque, there are no boundaries. Most of us would never have thought we could do what we do now, like wear a G-string onstage. But no one laughed at you, everybody was with you. So, after a year of creation, we became different people."

When the process works at its best, that person becomes the character audiences see onstage. Natasha Hallett, for instance, says: "I remember little things that Franco told me all the time when I'm onstage, like 'Always show the fire within.' Always have that fire within you that wants to come out. When you cross the line from backstage into the light, leave yourself back there, and become your character."

Tatiana Gousarova, an artist and gymnast who has appeared in *Quidam* and *Varekai*, puts it this way: "I trained for nine months with Franco. He was trying to find something unique in your personality, pushing for something he could use. Whatever it was, it was you. What that meant was that, onstage, it was easy. Whenever I went on stage, I felt I was being me."

Paul Bowler, who performs an aerial cube act in *Mystère*, sums it up: "Cirque transformed me into an artist. For the first twelve months, I was Paul Bowler with a cube. Hopefully, now, when you watch the act, it's Paul Bowler the Artist."

"WHEN YOU CROSS THE LINE FROM BACKSTAGE INTO THE LIGHT, LEAVE YOURSELF BACK THERE, AND BECOME YOUR CHARACTER."

A RUNAWAY SUCCESS

The results of this new wave of experimentation were indisputable. *Nouvelle Expérience* was a hit, touring North America throughout 1990 and 1991, and setting a new standard within the circus world.

Serge Roy, who acted as tour manager on *Nouvelle Expérience*, believes that the artistic and creative élan of the creative team, as well as its ideas, came to affect the company as a whole. "You could really feel the creative power coming out of that team," he remembers. "Franco's discourse was artistic, but it was philosophical at the same time, and it permeated the company."

By the end of 1990, Cirque du Soleil was profitable again, and would remain so. With *Nouvelle Expérience* up and running, the creative team resolved to continue exploring its methods in a new show. The name of that show, still running today, is *Saltimbanco*.

11/

09/
Nouvelle Expérience ARTISTS LES
FLOUNES. LEFT TO RIGHT: CÉCILE ARDAIL,
PATRICE WOJCIECHOWSKI, CHRISTOPHE
LELARGE, DAVID LEBEL, ISABELLE
CHASSÉ.

10/
CHARACTER SKETCHES, DOMINIQUE
LEMIEUX. IN THE CREATIVE PROCESS THAT
BEGAN IN EARNEST WITH *NOUVELLE
EXPÉRIENCE*, CIRQUE ARTISTS ARE
ENCOURAGED TO LOSE THEIR INHIBITIONS
AND EXPRESS THEIR INNER SELVES.

11/
ISABELLE CHASSÉ.

12/
JINNY JACINTO, ISABELLE CHASSÉ,
LAURENCE RACINE-CHOINIÈRE. MISSING
FROM PICTURE: NADINE LOUIS-BINETTE.

12/

SALTIMBANCO

EXPLORING URBAN LIFE

CHAPTER
8

> **IN THE CITY, YOU WILL FIND US**
> **NEITHER FANTASY NOR REALITY,**
> **NEITHER MAN NOR WOMAN,**
> **GOD NOR DEMON, SONG NOR STORY.**
> **WE ARE NO ONE, WE ARE LEGION**
> **WE ARE SALTIMBANCO!**

EXPLORING URBAN LIFE

Saltimbanco was launched in 1992. Twelve years later, the show is still on tour, having thrilled new audiences in North America, Europe, Japan, and Australia.

Saltimbanco was the first show in which Cirque du Soleil felt it could narrow its creative focus on a specific set of themes and ideas to feed its driving need to follow the "vague intuition."

Franco Dragone says, "The theme that guided me from the beginning of *Saltimbanco* was urbanism." Given the multicultural and rootless cosmopolitan nature of Cirque du Soleil, it's not surprising that the creative team chose to examine the potential of increasing urbanization.

For Guy Laliberté, the decision to explore urbanism came directly out of Cirque du Soleil's experience as touring entertainers.

"I'm a traveler, I'm aware of how the world is," Laliberté explains. "For me, *Saltimbanco* is a message of peace. In the 1990s, immigration was an issue, the mixing of cultures in cities, and *Saltimbanco* reflects that mix, with all of its personalities and colors. It's the challenge we have in today's world: respecting each other, living and working together, despite our differences."

"The cosmopolitan experience is at the root of this show," explains Michel Crête. "But the visions of urbanity that were around at the time were all variations on future dystopias, with echoes of the cold war, visions of the planet in danger. There weren't many reasons given for hope in a better tomorrow. We wanted to look at city life in a new way, we wanted to explore uncharted territory."

"THE COSMOPOLITAN EXPERIENCE

IS AT THE ROOT OF THIS SHOW."

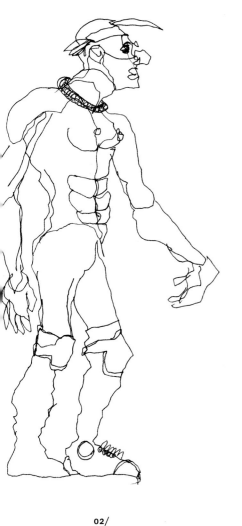

02/

Doing this entailed a certain amount of risk, according to Crête. "Cataclysms and catastrophes are always spectacular, in a way that optimism maybe isn't," he comments. "And yet, despite all the portents of doom and gloom hanging over our heads, there are still people of good will working to improve things, in a positive way, to make the future better."

The decision to explore urbanity in a positive light influenced everything from character creation and costume design to music and set design.

Speaking of her work, Dominique Lemieux says: "We wanted to do something simple, almost naïve in expression. That's how we came up with the 'Baroques' characters. The 'Vers Masqués' are like the mass of people you see in a city. If you look at them quickly, they all look the same. But when you look more closely, you see a baroque creature: a unique individual, sometimes even a bit of a monster, a monster with a heart." Seeing the potential for personal transformation in this duality, Lemieux adds, "We all want to come out of ourselves and become someone else."

The idea of lightness was a big influence on Michel Crête's set design. "I oriented my research toward building materials, the use of space," he explains. "I realized that people on the planet are working to improve the environment, for instance developing made-to-measure building materials, intended for a predetermined length of time, with a plan to recover and recycle those materials. People weren't just building nuclear warheads."

"There's an imperative in the manufacture of most things, including cars and airplanes, to make them lighter," he continues. "The idea of lightness leads to other ideas, like transparency. Utilitarian ideas like that naturally lead to esthetic preoccupations."

René Dupéré, once again asked to score the show, found the idea of urban life confounding at first. "The problem with the Cirque shows is that every act wants the best music in the show," he says. "Each piece of music has to be different, but the show needed a thread to unite everything. This was the first and biggest challenge: to put everything together so it wouldn't look like a mix of things that don't belong together. From that point of view, *Saltimbanco* was the most difficult show for me to do because there's so much difference from one theme to another."

Dupéré finally found a unifying idea when he wondered what it would be like to drive through a major city like New York. "The idea that I had was this," he recalls: "What would it sound like if I rode from one end of the city to another with the car window rolled down? I would hear everything from Jamaican to Classical music. It was a very simple idea: the idea that our urban life means the democratization of music, that everything is available. The twentieth century was the century of human memory. We had all the technology we needed to remember human history. That's what *Saltimbanco* was about for me."

A BAROQUE SHOW

From Franco Dragone's point of view, *Saltimbanco* was "baroque" in the sense described by a twentieth-century Italian poet named Giuseppe Ungaretti. "To Ungaretti," says Dragone, "'baroque' meant a desire to confront the Void, and to fill it so much that you feel life will never end. I wanted to fill the stage because I was afraid of the Void, of Nothingness."

01/
SANDRA FEUSI, THE BAROQUE DANDY.

02/
DOMINIQUE LEMIEUX. FROM THE BEGINNING, *SALTIMBANCO* WAS CONCEIVED AS A BAROQUE SHOW POPULATED BY CHARACTERS REFLECTING HUMAN DIVERSITY.

03/
SALTIMBANCO ARTIST ANATOLI BELIAEV REFLECTS BACKSTAGE.

"TO KEEP A SHOW RUNNING, YOU ALWAYS HAVE TO LOOK FOR ITS RELEVANCE IN A NEW SOCIETY."

PULLED OUT OF RETIREMENT

Saltimbanco's original run ended in 1997. In 1998, however, Cirque du Soleil decided to put it back on the road, to open new markets, beginning in Australia. As Lyn Heward explains, management at Cirque du Soleil felt *Saltimbanco* still had legs.

"To keep a show running, you always have to look for its relevance in a new society," says Heward. "Before we choose to send a show to a new place, we ask 'Is it still relevant?' Not only passable, but also *stimulating* in today's society. So far, with *Saltimbanco*, we haven't come to the conclusion that it's no longer relevant. Ultimately, it's the show's creators who make the decision. That buck will stop with Guy."

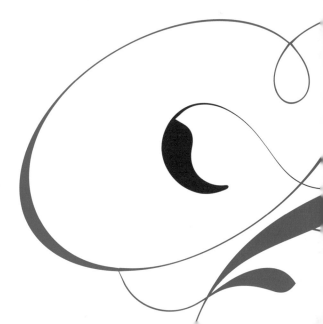

04/

04/
THE WORLD OF *SALTIMBANCO*.
CLOCKWISE FROM TOP LEFT: WANG
JINGMIN, THE DOUBLE WIRE; THE
DREAMER GENNADY CHIZHOV, LINDA
BÉLANGER AS THE CAVALIER OF LIGHT;
A VERS MASQUÉ.

"YOU GET CAUGHT BY A LOOK FROM SOMEONE IN THE AUDIENCE, AND YOU CONNECT. IT'S MAGIC."

A BIG, COLORFUL PARTY

Certainly, the show is still stimulating for members of its ever-changing and evolving cast, who speak of it in glowing terms. Isabelle Dansereau-Corradi, for instance, has sung with Cirque du Soleil in various shows since 1995. She singles out *Saltimbanco* as a favorite. "I switched over from *Alegría* because I like *Saltimbanco* a lot," she enthuses. "I also love to dance, and there's more movement in this show. There's a lot of freedom. I love it."

Carolyne Vita has performed with Cirque du Soleil since 1993, and is a vocal ambassador for the show. "I was in *Mystère* for five years," she says, "and I heard that *Saltimbanco* was starting out again. And I thought, 'Come on, I want to do *Saltimbanco*!' *Saltimbanco* has a lot of character work, and it's one of the only shows that allows you to be free within that character."

Describing that freedom and the potential it offers for audience interaction, Vita adds: "I love connection with people. It's my passion. You get caught by a look from someone in the audience, and you connect. It's magic."

05/
WANG JINGMIN PERFORMS
THE DOUBLE WIRE ACT.

06/
THE DUO TRAPEZE, PERFORMED BY ELSIE
ADELIA SMITH AND SERENITY SMITH
FORCHION.

05/

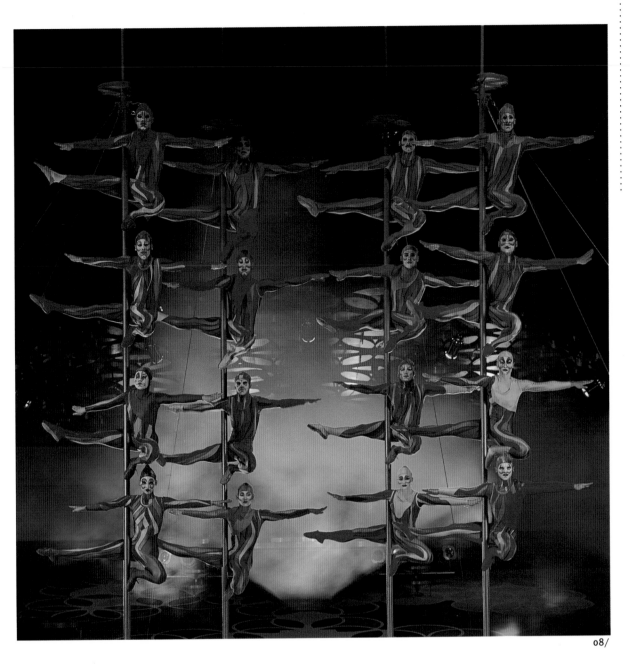

08/

07/08/
SALTIMBANCO'S HOUSE TROUPE PERFORM THE CHINESE POLES ACT (FROM TOP TO BOTTOM) 1ST POLE: JÉROME LE BAUT, MITCHELL HEAD, MARYIA USHENKA, CAROLYNE VITA. 2ND POLE: NICO KARSDORF, KRISTOFER CARRISON, WIESLAW MIECZYSLAW HACZKIEWICZ, ALEVTYNA TITARENKO. 3RD POLE: VITALII REDOUN, LAURENT MICHELIER, DARIN GOOD, LINDSAY ORTON. 4TH POLE: SAM PAYNE, ZBIGNIEW BACHOR, SANDRA FEUSI, MARIAN SORIN MALITA.

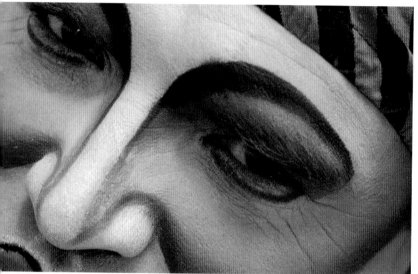

"*Saltimbanco* is a big, colorful party," she concludes. "We allow ourselves to do things that we aren't allowed to do in regular life, like sticking your tongue out at people, or blowing a stranger a kiss."

In the end, that connection—between artists, artists and their show, and artists and their audience—may be what keeps *Saltimbanco* fresh. Harking back to its original conception as an exploration of urban life, Guy Laliberté comments: "We rose to the challenge of living and working together, despite our differences, theatrically speaking. We have twelve, fourteen, fifteen different nationalities in every show. Not everyone speaks English—you have to find a way of working together. And yet, I'm always pleased to see the audience smiling and enjoying itself, and to realize that my gang has done it again."

"SALTIMBANCO IS A BIG, COLORFUL PARTY. WE ALLOW OURSELVES TO DO THINGS THAT WE AREN'T ALLOWED TO DO IN REGULAR LIFE, LIKE STICKING YOUR TONGUE OUT AT PEOPLE, OR BLOWING A STRANGER A KISS..."

09/

09/10/
SALTIMBANCO ARTISTS IN A FESTIVE MOOD, AS EVER, BACKSTAGE. OPPOSITE PAGE, FROM TOP: EDESIA MORENNO BARRATA, KRZYSZTOF BRUDNY; ELENA GROSCHEVA. THIS PAGE: LINDSAY ORTON.

10/

11/
THE BUNGEE ACT.

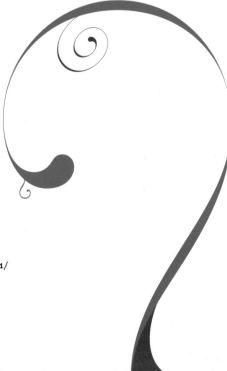

11/

THE UNKNOWN TURNING POINT:
FASCINATION

キリンラガー・ファシナシオン

WHILE IT WAS PREPARING FOR ITS LAUNCH OF SALTIMBANCO IN 1992, CIRQUE DU SOLEIL TOURED JAPAN FOR THE FIRST TIME WITH A SHOW COMBINING ACTS FROM LE CIRQUE RÉINVENTÉ AND NOUVELLE EXPÉRIENCE. DIRECTED BY GILLES STE-CROIX, IT WAS CALLED FASCINATION. THOUGH FASCINATION WAS NEVER SEEN OUTSIDE OF JAPAN, THE SHOW REPRESENTED ANOTHER IMPORTANT TURNING POINT FOR CIRQUE DU SOLEIL.

For the first time, Cirque had to learn how to work with a partner, in this case the Fuji Television Network. Dan Yoshida, who worked with Fuji, was instrumental in setting up the tour, which took place in arenas rather than under the big top. Fuji also helped Cirque adapt to its new audience.

Michael Rosenberger, an artist who has toured Japan, describes how different Japanese audiences can be. "In North America, audiences are the same, generally responsive," he says. "In Japan, audiences are very reserved, very polite. There's no cheering or getting excited or standing ovations for Japanese audiences. And yet they're excited inside. That's a bit of an adjustment. You wonder: 'My God, do they like us?' But then you learn that they appreciate the show in their way. They stay quiet and let you perform. We had to work pauses into the show, when the audience felt they could clap, because, if we didn't, they would never clap, even at the end."

Fuji provided detailed input as to what should be changed for the Japanese audience.

In the end, *Fascination* was a transforming experience for Cirque on two fronts. On the first, the show broadened Cirque's familiarity with the subtle differences between audiences around the world, making it an international entertainer in the truest sense. At the same time, it proved that Cirque du Soleil could work with powerful partners, setting the stage for future partnerships with MGM Mirage and The Walt Disney Company.

CHAPTER

9

MYSTÈRE

PLANTING A FLOWER IN THE DESERT

> JOURNEY TO THE VERY HEART OF LIFE
> WHERE PAST, PRESENT, AND FUTURE MERGE,
> WHERE EMOTIONS COLLIDE
> AND THE DEEP ENIGMA OF TIME UNFOLDS.
> HOPES, DREAMS, AND QUESTIONS AWAIT
> WHERE LIFE FOLLOWS ITS RELENTLESS,
> UNSTOPPABLE COURSE.

ON DECEMBER 25, 1993, SIX MONTHS SHY OF ITS TENTH ANNIVERSARY, CIRQUE DU SOLEIL BROKE NEW GROUND YET AGAIN, WITH THE PREMIERE OF *MYSTÈRE*. *MYSTÈRE* MARKED YET ANOTHER TURNING POINT, AS CIRQUE ESTABLISHED ITS FIRST RESIDENT SHOW IN LAS VEGAS.

PLANTING A FLOWER IN THE DESERT

In 1992, *Nouvelle Expérience* played a year-long run under the Grand Chapiteau in The Mirage parking lot. The success of that run led to a deal between Cirque and Steve Wynn, then Chairman, and Robert H. Baldwin, President, of The Mirage Casino-Hotel for a permanent show in Vegas.*

Running a permanent show would be an entirely new experience for Cirque. For the first time, it would have to face the logistical hurdles of setting up a permanent show infrastructure outside of Montreal, affecting everything from casting to lodging for artists and crew. It would also have to deal with the realities of building a theater as well as a show. All the time, it would have to remain creatively focused and strong.

Cirque responded to the challenges of setting up a permanent home in Las Vegas with a creative mission statement. With *Mystère*, they said, they would "plant a flower in the desert."

*NOTE: IN LATER YEARS, THE MIRAGE CASINO-HOTEL WOULD BE ACQUIRED BY MGM GRAND INC., WITH WHOM CIRQUE HAS A CONTINUING PARTNERSHIP UNDER ITS NEW NAME, MGM MIRAGE.

A FLOWER
IN THE DESERT

IS LAS VEGAS READY?

The resident show that became *Mystère* had been in the works years earlier, originally intended for Caesars Palace. Accordingly, it had been planned around themes from Greek and Roman mythology. Plans for that show were eventually scrapped, however, perhaps because Las Vegas was not yet ready for what Cirque du Soleil had to offer.

Describing Las Vegas circa 1990, Michel Crête says: "Vegas . . . was still very influenced by Les Folies Bergères, with the scarves, feather boas, etc. There was a European culture already in place, oddly enough, not an American one.

"The people who opened the door to something new were Siegfried and Roy. They were the first to move away from the Folies Bergères thing."

Guy Laliberté recalls that, while the people behind the Caesars Palace project were ready for change, they weren't ready for *too much* change. "*Mystère* was developed for Caesars Palace," he recalls, "but during a presentation to the board, they said it would be too risky and esoteric for a town like Las Vegas. We ended up doing it three years later at Treasure Island."

02/

"OUR SOURCES OF INSPIRATION FOR EACH SHOW ARE ALWAYS THREEFOLD: SOCIAL AND POLITICAL LIFE, OUR ARTISTIC HERITAGE AND QUOTIDIAN LIVES, AND THE INSTITUTIONAL LIFE OF CIRQUE DU SOLEIL. MYSTÈRE WAS ABOUT OUR PREOCCUPATION WITH THE UNIVERSE."

EXPLORING THE MYSTERIES OF THE UNIVERSE

During the move from Caesars Palace to Treasure Island, *Mystère* was transformed from a show about Greek and Roman mythology to a show about the origins of life in the universe. Describing its genesis, Franco Dragone says: "Our sources of inspiration for each show are always threefold: social and political life, our artistic heritage and quotidian lives, and the institutional life of Cirque du Soleil. *Mystère* was about our preoccupation with the universe."

Exploring the mystery of life led Dragone and costume designer Dominique Lemieux to populate the stage with figures from the plant and animal world. "While I was working on *Mystère*, I was really tripping on nature books," says Lemieux. "I was into chaos theory, and this extremely close-up nature photography. It had a huge effect on me. So the characters were half human, half animal. The first photographs that I put together in research were of many different areas across the planet. I was trying to bring together these colors and textures to have an idea of what we have around us, on earth. It brought me closer to birth, to animals and birds of paradise. There are a lot of animals in *Mystère*. It's a little like a jungle."

Dragone, too, recalls being influenced by chaos theory, with its attendant philosophical and theological implications. "The Butterfly Effect comes from chaos theory. It's about how a tiny effect can have a huge impact on the planet, how a butterfly flapping its wings here can have a cataclysmic effect in Australia," he says. "Chaos theory was in the air at the time, in a book by a man called Prigogine, a Russian scientist who was living in Belgium, and who won the Nobel Prize," Dragone adds. "The theory struck me with the question: Are things random, or are they not random? Does God play dice with the universe, or not?"

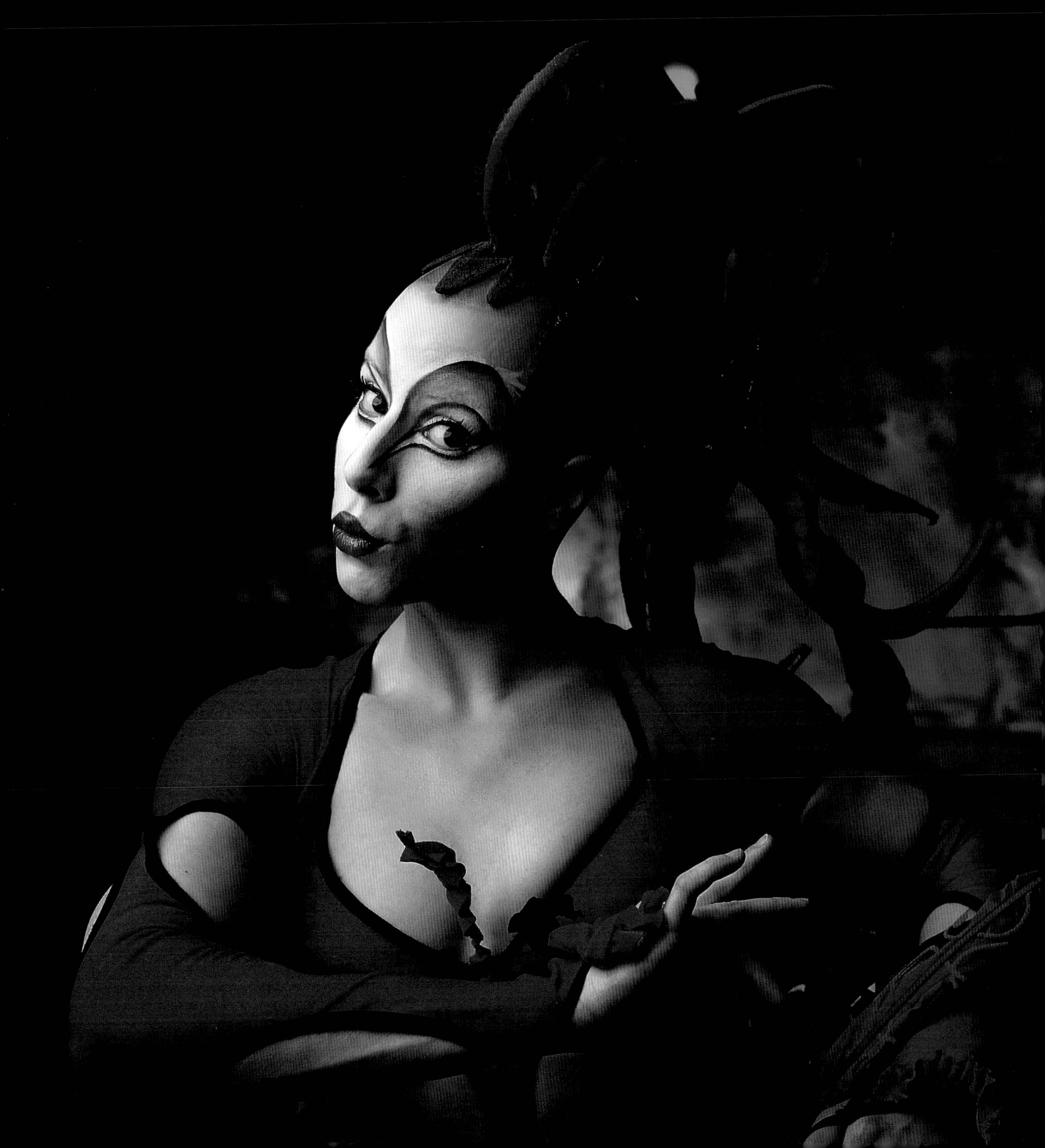

04/
ARTISTS PERFORM *MYSTÈRE*. FROM TOP
TO BOTTOM: CHINESE POLES; PAUL
BOWLER, THE AERIAL CUBE; THE CAST
TAKE A BOW.

05/
SÉBASTIEN COIN, THE YELLOW BIRD.

04/

"MYSTÈRE WAS ABOUT HOW LIFE CAME TO THE PLANET. IT'S THE STORY OF THE UNIVERSE THROUGH ALL THE MYTHOLOGIES."

05/

A VOYAGE INTO MYTH

While it explored new areas, the show retained elements of mythology. "*Mystère* was about how life came to the planet," remembers Dragone, drawing a link. "It's the story of the universe through all the mythologies. It sounds big and pretentious, but it helped us construct images that came from the plant world, a universe filled with the monsters of childhood."

"*Mystère* is an initiation," he continues, "a voyage of initiation for this Baby who confronts different worlds, different rites of passage. He's confronted by these things that are titanic in size, because, sometimes, things are too big for us to understand."

06/
MYSTÈRE'S GIANT SNAIL, A PUPPET,
COULD REPRESENT THE MYSTERIOUSLY
SLOW, IMMENSE PASSAGE OF TIME.

07/
LA PLUME, CHARACTER
DESIGN BY DOMINIQUE LEMIEUX.

08/
MARCO AND PAOLO LORADOR PERFORM
THE HAND-TO-HAND ACT.

09/
MAGALIE DROLET, AS ONE OF
THE PAGNES, PLAYS THE TAIKO DRUMS.

10/
PHILIPPA HAYBALL, GREEN LIZARD.
MYSTÈRE PRESENTS A WORLD WHERE
ANIMAL, PLANT, AND HUMAN BECOME ONE.

11/
LA MOUCHE, ANOTHER
MYTHOLOGICAL CHARACTER SKETCHED
BY DOMINIQUE LEMIEUX.

10/

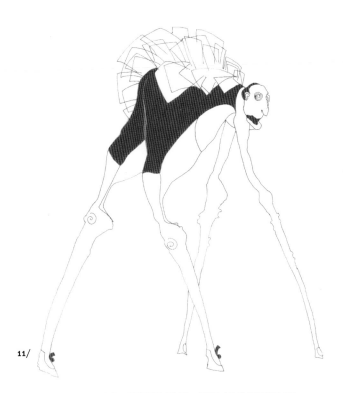

11/

WORKING UNDER PRESSURE

Michel Crête is extremely reluctant to talk about *Mystère*. "*Mystère* was our first time in a theater, and I have to admit that I really wasn't ready for the realities we had to adapt to," he says.

The creative team was under tremendous pressure with *Mystère*. For the first time, it had to work with a major financial partner in the form of Mirage Casino-Hotel. Clashes between the team's freeform methods and Mirage's more traditional business structure were inevitable.

Nevertheless, Crête will speak about the mythical elements retained in the set design. "We were influenced by mythology,' Crête confirms. "For me, the sky in the set is an archaic sky. And there's Caryb and Scylla."

"Caryb" and "Scylla" are the two rock formations on either side of the *Mystère* stage. René Dupéré, who also took Greek mythology as his cue in scoring the show, explains: "Caryb and Scylla are two rocks in a strait between Europe and Africa. There's a saying: 'to go from Caryb to Scylla,' which means to go from bad to worse."

MOVING IN A WORLD-BEAT DIRECTION

Influenced by mythology, Dupéré decided to explore what he calls an "ethnic" direction in his score. "For me, *Mystère* is the most ethnic music that I wrote for Cirque. My 'ethnic' music has two different flavors, either Spanish/African, or flavors from the Balkans and eastern countries."

Mystère was the first show since 1986 that Dupéré did not compose in its entirety. "I composed the whole show at the beginning," he specifies, "but then Benoit Jutras had to compose a lot of music when they changed a few numbers and I wasn't available."

According to Benoit Jutras, who had been a bandleader with Cirque until that point, the mythical impetus pushed Cirque du Soleil's music even more decidedly toward world beat. "I think that *Mystère* was really the end of an era that included *Le Cirque réinventé*, *Nouvelle Expérience*, and *Saltimbanco*, and the beginning of another era," Jutras says. "You still hear a lot of new age/rock like they had in the first shows, and that you hear less of in the shows after that. At the same time, you start to hear more and more world-beat influences."

"PEOPLE BRING THEIR OWN WAYS OF MOVING AND THEIR OWN PERSONALITIES INTO THE CHARACTER THEY'RE PLAYING, SO THE CHARACTER BECOMES SOMETHING DIFFERENT."

WORKING WITH GYMNASTS

Mystère's acrobatic skeleton required a higher level of gymnastic skill than any other Cirque production before it. Increasingly, Cirque would come to scout national and Olympic-level gymnasts for its shows.

According to Lyn Heward, this represented a clash of cultures that was not easy to manage. "I found it very difficult," she recalls, "because, at the time, we had gymnasts who were from, mostly, Britain, Canada, and the United States, versus circus performers who had really been brought up in the French circus school tradition. And I'll never forget the day when Nordine, who was a French circus performer, got so frustrated that he put his head through the plasterboard wall of the studio. 'I can't work like a gymnast,' he said, 'I feel like I'm in the Army, or the Air Force or something. It's too regimented! That's not how the circus arts evolved!'"

From the beginning, however, the creative team saw the potential of working with gymnasts. Dominique Lemieux, for instance, says, "The casting for *Mystère* was really excellent. The cast had a lot of dramatic potential, a lot of presence. We saw what they could become, and what they wanted to become."

As the show has evolved, many gymnasts have found their comfort zone in the show, and used it as an opportunity to develop as artists. Natasha Hallett is a prime example.

"The show has evolved a lot," Hallett says. "People bring their own ways of moving and their own personalities into the character they're playing, so the character becomes something different."

Describing her own role in the show, Hallett continues: "I'm the FireBird. I'm a loner. I'm a troublemaker. I come and go as I please. I was part of the house troupe* before, and I was always getting into trouble for being different. I couldn't fit into the mold. The artistic directors picked up on that, and suggested I become a character. They weren't satisfied with the guy who was playing the Firebird before, and it had always been a guy character, never a girl. I thought: 'They'll never go for a girl as that character.' For one thing, it meant completely changing the costume. The costume was open in front. But, in 1999, they suggested I go for it."

Ultimately, according to Paul Bowler, the ability of the gymnasts/artists to evolve within the show ultimately pays off for the audience. Bowler, who performs *Mystère*'s Aerial Cube Act, explains: "Fifty percent of my act is gymnastics, but I try to bring it as far away from gymnastics as possible. I don't want to have 1,600 people watching me do gymnastics. I want them to see an artist, something they haven't seen before, that they can relate to, or not relate to. Like, 'How does he do that? How is that possible?' An entrepreneur might watch us and go, 'Oh, I could do that.' Another guy watching will see things another way. It's all about relating and communicating."

*NOTE: Members of the house troupe are Cirque artists who appear in more than one act, and who often play more than one role, as opposed to "invited guest artists," performers with a preexisting act fitted into a particular show.

14/

12/
SÉBASTIEN COIN, THE YELLOW BIRD,
HANDBALANCING.

13/14/
NICHOLAS DEWHURST AS MOHA-SAMEDI
(LEFT) AND HIS FATHER, BRIAN
DEWHURST, AS BRIAN LE PETIT (RIGHT).
THE DEWHURSTS HAVE BEEN CIRCUS
PERFORMERS FOR GENERATIONS.

WINNING OVER VEGAS

These days, the success of *Mystère* is inarguable. And yet, as its premiere approached in 1993, the show's backer Steve Wynn was less than convinced about its prospects. "After he saw *Mystère* for the first time," remembers Guy Laliberté, "Steve Wynn said, 'You guys have made a German opera here.' Franco answered, 'You just gave me the best compliment I've ever heard.'"

Despite Wynn's initial misgivings, *Mystère* continues to win over audiences. "It really opened things up in terms of the type of show you could see in Las Vegas," Laliberté says. "That feels really good."

Cirque had come through its first experience of building a permanent show with flying colors. It was ready for its next challenge, a show that would test Cirque du Soleil's capacity to explore darkness as well as light: *Alegría*.

"IT REALLY OPENED THINGS UP IN TERMS OF THE TYPE OF SHOW YOU COULD SEE IN LAS VEGAS. THAT FEELS REALLY GOOD.

15/
THE HOUSE TROUPE.

16/
THE OPERATIC CHANTEUSE PLUME, AS CONCEIVED BY DOMINIQUE LEMIEUX.

16/

CHAPTER
10

ALEGRÍA

POWER IN THE BALANCE

> MAY **ALEGRÍA** BECOME A RALLYING CRY
FOR YOUNG HEARTS FROZEN IN THE GUTTER
FOR THOSE WHO KNOW NO LAUGHTER.
IF YOU HAVE NO VOICE, SCREAM.
IF YOU HAVE NO LEGS, RUN.
IF YOU HAVE NO HOPE, INVENT
ALEGRÍA!

ALEGRÍA, AN OPERATIC MEDITATION ON THE ABUSES OF POWER AND THE PURGING ENERGY OF YOUTH, WAS LAUNCHED IN 1994. IT HAS TOURED CONSTANTLY SINCE—INCLUDING A YEAR-LONG RESIDENCY AT BEAU RIVAGE, A RESORT IN BILOXI, MISSISSIPPI.

A CRY FROM THE HEART

According to Franco Dragone, *Alegría* was born of pain and frustration. "*Mystère* had really been a battleground," he explains. "I don't know if it's because we were dealing with chaos as a theme, but it really was chaotic. It's the first show we did in a theater. No one in Cirque du Soleil had ever done that. The shows had always been presented under a big top. Just as we were really getting to understand the big top, *pow!*, we were doing a show in a theater."

Dragone explains that adapting technical demands to the artistic potential of the theater created problems. "Everything that happens on a stage has nothing to do with what happens under a big top," he says. "Under a big top, you can bring in acrobatic equipment and say, 'Okay, we'll be performing on this equipment.' But if you bring a trampoline out onto a stage, it means something else. It's hard to get technical people to understand that. It sounds silly, but you can't bring on a teeterboard and just bring it on as teeterboard. Maybe you have to put wheels on it, so it can be a chariot that you use in a scene. I found it hard to deal with."

01-02/
CINDY WHITEMAN, NYMPH.
ALEGRÍA WAS CONCEIVED AS A SHOW
THAT WOULD TAKE AUDIENCES ON A
JOURNEY THROUGH DARKNESS TO LIGHT.

02/

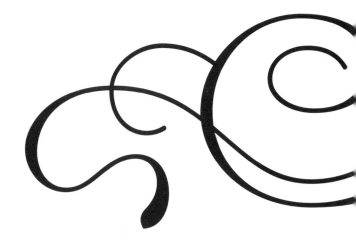

THAT TENSION BETWEEN THE ABUSE OF POWER AND THE STRUGGLE FOR FREEDOM

The idea of *Alegría* struck Dragone as he confronted these problems. "While all that was happening, we were already thinking about the next show," he says. "At one point, I was with Guy Laliberté at a restaurant in one of the Las Vegas casinos, and I told him the next show would be sad, heavy, really hard: 'Alegría! Alegría! Alegría!' It's Italian for 'Joy! Joy! Joy!' Where I come from, it's what you say when you're in pain. It means life goes on. *Alegría*, life goes on, *Alegría!*

"That's where the title came from. First we had the title, and then we came up with the rest of the show."

03/

04/

ALEGRÍA, IT'S WHAT YOU SAY WHEN YOU'RE IN PAIN. IT MEANS LIFE GOES ON. ALEGRÍA, LIFE GOES ON, ALEGRÍA!

03/
ALEXANDRE DOBRYNINE, FLYING MAN.

04/
TAMIR ERDENESAIKHAN AND BATMUNKH
BATJARGAL AS TAMIR AND LITTLE TAMIR.

05/
FRONT TO BACK: GEORGE-ÉTIENNE,
VALENTIN AND PIGRETTE, GRACIEUSE,
AND ALEXI AS THE NOSTALGIC OLD BIRD
CHARACTERS.

THE WEIGHT OF OPPRESSION

Michel Crête remembers his inspiration for *Alegría* coming from a deeply upsetting real-life event. "While we were putting the show together," he remembers, "this very young boy was kidnapped and killed by two other boys in England, and we couldn't get over it. I remember thinking, 'How can a human being pretend to have the right to exercise such power over another human being?' What really struck me was that it was *children* acting in such an evil way. For me, *Alegría* is really about the abuse of power."

The weight of power clearly influenced Crête's set design. "*Alegría* is the opposite of *Saltimbanco*. Where *Saltimbanco* was about lightness, this was all about heaviness. There's a lot of influence from Gothic arches, which for me are all about oppressive power."

Alegría became a show about both the abuse of power and the weight of powerlessness, and their opposite—the possibility of liberation. For Dominique Lemieux, that possibility was profound, and an instinctual part of the creative process. "It's strange to say," she recalls, "but I drew *Alegría* in my gut. I can see it: I see an egg, in a kind of cage, and, inside it, a very tiny, very fragile life. *Alegría*'s a scream, but not of joy. It's more of a decision to fight for life."

That tension between the abuse of power and the struggle for freedom took on a broader political dimension. In a way, it also came to reflect the relationship between audience and performer. Franco Dragone explains: "... in our relations with the powers-that-be, we always say: 'Damn, our leaders are no good, they're this, they're that.' But if they weren't there, I think we'd run around like chickens with our heads cut off, we'd be lost. There's a relationship between the king and the fool: they're interdependent. Without the fool, there's no king. Without the king, there's no fool. And we, as nomadic street performers, we're like society's fool, we can help society move forward. It's a dialogue."

The relationship between king and fool became composer René Dupéré's main inspiration. "I started from a single idea that came from Gilles Ste-Croix and Franco: the idea that the fools have lost their king," Dupéré recalls. "For me, the fool and the king can be two parts of the same individual, mirroring one another. It gave a sort of half-ethnic, half-middle-ages feel to parts of the music."

05/

ALEGRÍA PITS THE POWERFUL AGAINST THE POWERLESS, THE KING AGAINST HIS FOOLS, THE OLD AGAINST THE YOUNG.

DEALING WITH DUALITIES

Alegría pits the powerful against the powerless, the king against his fools, the old against the young.

"The Nostalgic Old Birds represent the palsied establishment," explains Michel Crête. "They don't do anything, they don't produce anything, and yet they have power over life and death."

"We saw the Nostalgic Old Birds as ancient characters, old, dusty, full of pride, with every fault imaginable," elaborates Dominique Lemieux. "You can catch those faults like a disease: they have them all and cherish them. They have beautifully decorated costumes, but inside, *Alegría* is like the little grain of purity that's left, the inner child that's still there."

"*Alegría*," she continues, "is the force inside every individual that allows them to resist corruption: *Alegría*'s a path, like a scream that gives us the strength to keep living no matter what happens to us." Some characters, like the Angels and the Bronx, are clearly on that opposing, liberating path.

Dragone's casting choices seem to suggest that these dualities ultimately exist within everyone. Danielle Rodenkirchen, who was in the original cast, explains: "In *Alegría*, Franco found a devil and an angel in all of us. I was one of the Nostalgic Old Birds. I also did the Fast Track—two extremes."

Alegría contrasts light and darkness, despair and hope, age and youth. Pierre Parisien, the artistic director of both *Alegría* and *Quidam* at publication, reaffirms the contrasts, saying, "*Alegría* is a sad show in its tone. It makes me think of autumn. But the spirit of the show is joyful, because of the youth and beauty."

PERHAPS ALEGRÍA HAS LASTED SO LONG BECAUSE—WITH ITS MIX OF OLD AND NEW, POWER AND FREEDOM, DARKNESS AND LIGHT—IT IS TIMELESS.

08/

THE CIRCUS, OLD AND NEW

Steeped in nostalgia, *Alegría* harks back to an older circus tradition. Oddities walk the stage, like the sideshow freaks of older times. "The circus tradition," underlines Michel Crête, "has always confronted people with the monstrous and fantastic." Mingled among them, stock circus characters like the Strong Man appear.

At the same time, however, the show is innovative, and constantly renewed. *Alegría*, for example, represents the first time that the Fast Track—a series of connected trampolines embedded in the main stage—was ever used. With the Fast Track in place, the tumbling act featuring the Bronx characters could be integrated into the show without the need to bring complicated equipment on and off the stage.

In the years since its premiere, explains Pierre Parisien, the show has been kept ever fresh: "The rhythm of the show has become much tighter. Fast Track, Russian Bars . . . all of the acts are tighter and more acrobatic."

Perhaps *Alegría* has lasted so long because—with its mix of old and new, power and freedom, darkness and light—it is timeless.

08/
BATMUNKH BATJARGAL, LITTLE TAMIR.
ALEGRÍA EMBRACES DUALITY, WITH BOTH
SHADOWS AND LIGHT.

09/
SKETCHES BY DOMINIQUE LEMIEUX.

10/
EBON GRAYMAN AS FLEUR LEADS THE
OLD NOSTALGIC BIRDS IN A PROCESSION.

09/

"THE CIRCUS TRADITION HAS ALWAYS CONFRONTED PEOPLE WITH THE MONSTROUS AND **FANTASTIC.**"

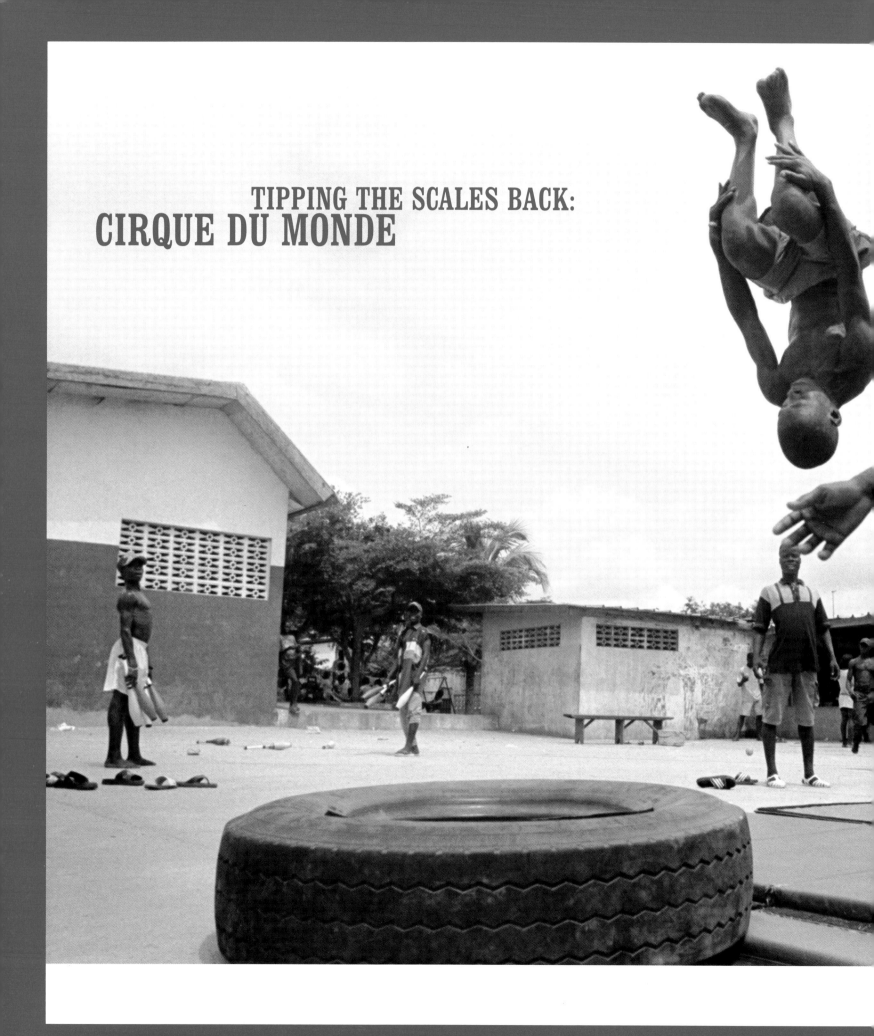

TIPPING THE SCALES BACK:
CIRQUE DU MONDE

CIRQUE DU SOLEIL'S CONCERN ABOUT SOCIAL INEQUALITY DIDN'T BEGIN WITH ALEGRÍA. IN FACT, CIRQUE HAS ALWAYS TRIED TO MAKE THE WORLD A BETTER PLACE. "WE'RE FROM THE STREETS," SAYS GUY LALIBERTÉ. "WE DON'T WANT TO FORGET WHERE WE'RE FROM. WHEN WE LIVED IN THE STREETS, IT TOUCHED US TO SEE YOUNG PEOPLE WITH NO FUTURE, WHO THOUGHT SO LITTLE OF THEMSELVES." LOOKING BACK TO HIS OWN UPBRINGING, HE ADDS: "I WAS FORTUNATE. I HAD LOVING PARENTS. I HAD A GOOD HOME. I ALWAYS KNEW I'D HAVE THREE MEALS A DAY AND A ROOF OVER MY HEAD. THE REST HAS BEEN A GIFT FROM LIFE. BUT I KNEW THERE WERE A LOT OF PEOPLE WHO HAD IT WORSE."

14/

In 1993, Cirque decided to target its goodwill efforts toward young people in difficulty, out of its deep-seated collective belief in the ability of youth to invent, create, and imagine. In 1994, Cirque du Soleil's tenth anniversary, Cirque du Monde was created to consolidate these activities.

Cirque du Monde works with young people at the local and international levels. In locations throughout the world, Cirque du Monde provides circus arts workshops to youth at risk, through community organizations. Paul Laporte, of Cirque's Social Affairs and International Cooperation Department, says, "At this very moment, nearly two billion children and young people all over the world are excluded, living on the margins of society. We want governments to be aware of the situation and to do something about it."

"I think it's our responsibility as shapers of opinion and as a successful company to do something," emphasizes Guy Laliberté. "We have to do what we can to make the world a better place. It's our social responsibility to nurture the circle of life that way."

Cirque du Monde was created in cooperation with Jeunesse du Monde, a nonprofit organization whose mission is to support people in disadvantaged countries fighting for survival, social justice, and human rights.

Since 1994, several hundred young people have taken part in Cirque du Monde workshops in the United States, Canada, Brazil, Colombia, the Netherlands, and Singapore. About thirty coaches and performers from Cirque du Soleil have also participated in the program. Any artist or coach who wants to donate time to the cause is encouraged to do so, and can take a year's sabbatical with Cirque du Monde if they choose.

"We can help get these people moving in a better direction by working on their self-esteem," says a deeply committed Laliberté. "It's the foundation that will give them the ability to dream."

Cirque's commitment to social action is backed by corporate policy. "One percent of our gross revenue is dedicated to social action," specifies C.O.O. Daniel Lamarre. "*Gross*, not net. The more we grow, the larger that dedication grows."

Ten years and counting later, Cirque du Monde is working beyond Laliberté's expectations. "I really saw the impact it's had in Brazil," he says. "I travel to Brazil a lot. I've been going for twenty years, and I visit Rio regularly."

"There are certain street corners where, for years, you would see young people who had been sniffing glue, their eyes glazed over, begging. Some of the first Cirque du Monde programs were in Rio. About two or three years ago, on the same street corner, you could see that something had happened. The same young people were asking for money—but they were juggling while they did it. So instead of begging, they're performing, they're doing something to earn it."

16/

"WE CAN HELP GET THESE PEOPLE MOVING IN A BETTER DIRECTION BY WORKING ON THEIR SELF-ESTEEM, IT'S THE FOUNDATION THAT WILL GIVE THEM THE ABILITY TO DREAM."

QUIDAM
SPEAKING FOR THE VOICELESS

➤ **THE NAMELESS AND SOLITARY PASSERBY, THE FACELESS STRANGER RUSHING PAST, LOST IN THE SMOTHERING CROWD LOOKING FOR THE COURAGE TO RIP HER SOUL FREE.**

In 1996, Cirque du Soleil premiered *Quidam* in Montreal. It is a darker show than any before or since, telling the story of a lonely girl and the crowd of quidams (faceless individuals) around her. For some, *Quidam* is the most stripped-down and nakedly human show in Cirque's oeuvre. Subversive and underground in spirit, it suggests that even lost souls can be set free by imagination.

The show was born out of Franco Dragone's desire to move away from the more fantastic textures of Cirque's previous shows to something more grounded in realism. In doing so, he hoped to get back to the feeling of uncertainty and danger that had always propelled Cirque creatively.

"I wanted to shake Cirque du Soleil up, to make us feel a little insecure, so we could continue to feel wonder and be audacious," he remembers. "We didn't always need color and beauty. We were tired of creating beautiful characters, angels, demons, nostalgic birds. I wanted to explore the anonymous mass of people, all those people we don't know. There are six billion quidams on the planet. I know maybe one hundred. That still leaves billions that I don't know, all of them quidams, unknowns, nobodies. I wanted to see life through their eyes."

In Guy Laliberté's words, *Quidam* is "a tribute to the faceless people you don't get to know."

THROUGH THE EYES OF A CHILD

In working out their approach, the creative team decided that the best way to tell that story would be through the eyes of a young girl. "I drew a character with its arms in the air," says Dominique Lemieux, remembering the moment the idea first came to her. "As soon as I saw the character," she continues, "it made me think of the fragility of childhood, the fragility of adolescence discovering the world as it is."

"It was interesting to consider the world through the eyes of a ten-year-old girl today," recalls Franco. "What is her day like? She wakes up, she turns on the TV, and zaps through the war in the Middle East, Disneyland, economic problems. . . . Fairy tales are not the same now. If you're a ten-year-old girl, you're already facing what an adult has to face. You're becoming older faster. Some kids already have weapons in their hands, and are fighting for food."

02/

01/
THE FACELESS **QUIDAM** WALKS A WORLD
OF ANONYMOUS CHARACTERS.

02/
FOR *QUIDAM*, DOMINIQUE LEMIEUX WAS
INSPIRED BY SURREALIST PAINTERS
MAGRITTE AND DELVEAUX.

03/
THE AVIATOR, ALEXANDRE LEONTIEV.

03/

04/

05/

INSPIRED BY SURREALISTS

Working out a visual signature for the show, Dragone and Lemieux were influenced by the surrealist movement in painting—particularly with its undercurrent of alienation.

"I'm from Italy, but I lived in Belgium, and I loved the Belgian surrealist movement," explains Dragone. "There were lots of painters, one in particular that I liked called Delveaux. In his paintings you see lots of people, and yet each painting communicates a kind of sadness between all those people. I wondered, 'Why?' When I looked more closely at the paintings, I could see that no one was looking at anyone else. If you look at *Quidam,* that's kind of the story, too."

"Delveaux inspired me . . . Magritte, too" says Dominique Lemieux, citing another influence. "Delveaux has a kind of sadness. It's a little like the attitude that parents have. You're an adolescent, and you feel like your parents aren't there. They're there, but they're not there. It's a kind of solitude."

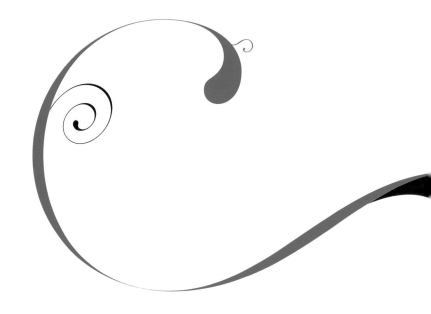

MAKING A VIRTUE OF NECESSITY

Following the incorporation of the Fast Track into the *Alegria* set, *Quidam* would be an even bolder step forward in integrating acrobatic equipment into the show's dramatic and thematic flow. Michel Crête remembers that the effort was born of practical necessity.

"In our previous shows, there was a lot of time spent mounting and dismounting the acrobatic equipment on stage," Crête remembers. "Franco and I wanted to find a way to incorporate the equipment into the set, so there would be more time and room for Franco to work out his staging. We wanted more room to work."

Crête designed an overhead rigging structure that would allow the artists to enter and exit from above and across the stage. Seeing it opened up design possibilities that deepened *Quidam*'s existential undercurrent. "When we saw the structure we'd invented, the notion of a railway station presented itself," Crête explains. "We found the idea interesting because, one, it's a meeting place, and two, it's also a place where you make life-changing decisions. You take one train or another, you can change your life's direction."

TOO DARK?

Some who may have grown used to the sunnier shades and brighter colors of shows like *Saltimbanco* originally found *Quidam* too dark.

Gilles Ste-Croix remembers encountering such resistance at a *Quidam* marketing meeting, after the show's premiere. "Charles Zuckow, who was responsible for selling the show in San Francisco, was there," Ste-Croix remembers. "He'd been with us since 1988, and he said: 'This show is very dark. It's not really Cirque du Soleil. I don't know if I can sell this.'"

Ste-Croix was nonplussed. "I said, 'Well, we're sold out in Montreal,'" he recalls with a smile. "Eventually, we sold out in San Francisco, too. I bug Charlie about it every time I see him."

10/

TOUCHING A HUMAN CHORD

In Cirque's twentieth year, *Quidam* toured Japan. Despite its darker shadings, it continues to appeal to fans. *Quidam* artistic director Pierre Parisien believes it's because the show is so human.

"For me, *Quidam* is about human beings, even if the treatment is surrealistic," he says. "Fifty percent of the original cast is still with the show. They love it, because the characters they are playing are real human beings."

Parisien says that because his artists are so committed to *Quidam*, they keep developing the show's emotional core. "The artists feel the show more as it goes along," he says. "They've internalized it more."

THE TRANSFORMING POWER OF CREATIVITY

Ultimately, *Quidam* is a show rooted in hope.

"*Quidam* could be seen as heavy," Parisien explains, "but all of our shows give hope. And the hope comes from *creativity*." That creativity can touch its audience in a profound way, he continues. "I like to think, when people come to see us, that at least one person will see the show and decide to be better. Because they'll tell themselves: 'If these people can create a show like this, I can do something better with my life. I can be a better person.'"

11/
MARIE-ÊVE BISSON, MARIE-MICHÈLE
FABER, AND ALOYSIA GAVRE PERFORM
THE AERIAL HOOP ACT.

12/
TOP CENTER: FAON BÉLANGER AND
SHAYNE COURTRIGHT. TOP RIGHT:
NICOLLE LIQUORISH. TOP LEFT: NATALIA
PESTOVA. BOTTOM: JASON PAPP,
MIREILLE GOYETTE, JONATHAN MORIN,
SPANISH WEBS

"WHEN WE SAW THE STRUCTURE WE'D INVENTED, THE NOTION OF A RAILWAY STATION PRESENTED ITSELF."

LIFE ON THE ROAD:
THE CIRQUE FAMILY

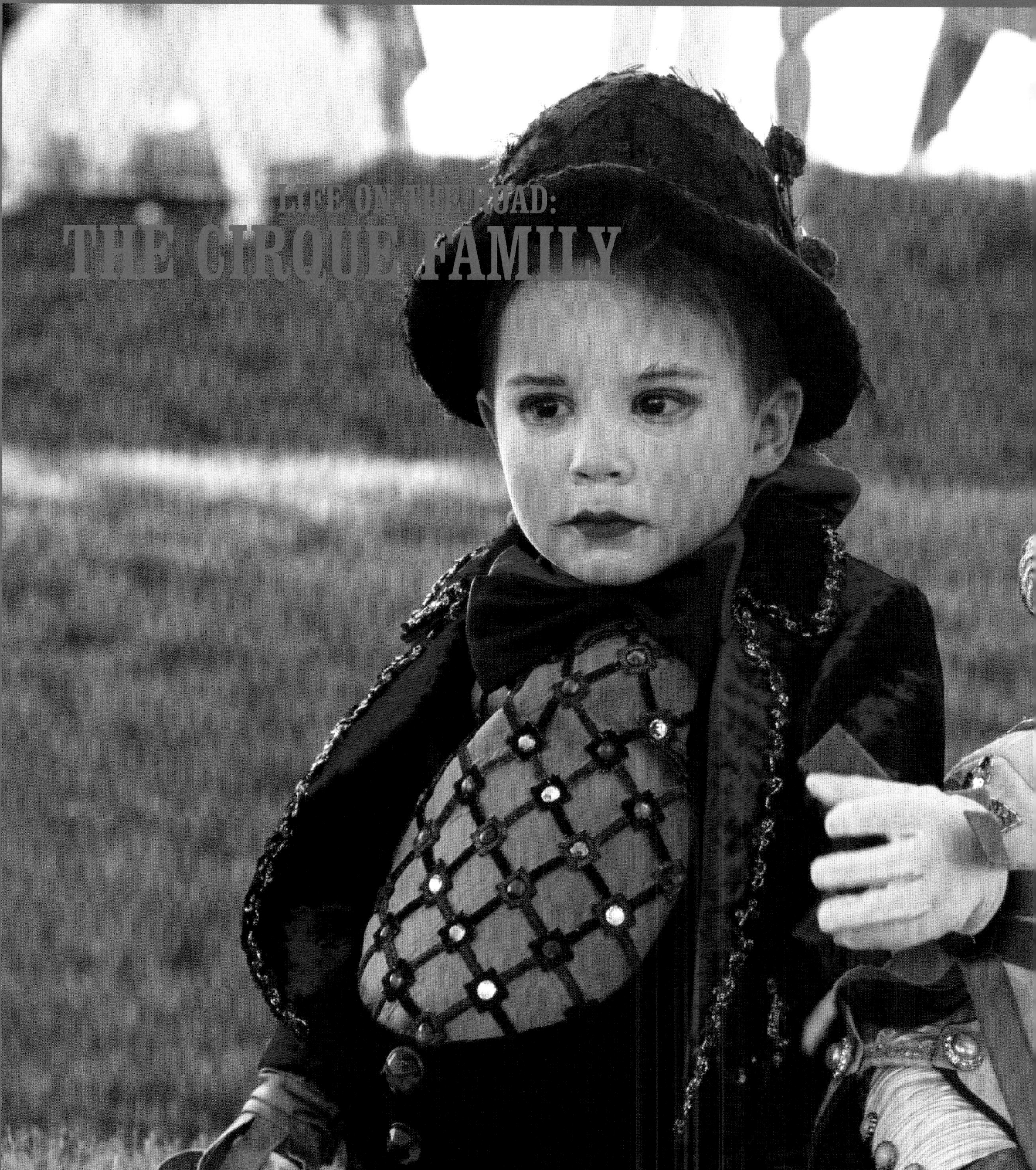

WHEN WE WALK INTO CIRQUE DU SOLEIL'S GRAND CHAPITEAU, WE ENTER ANOTHER WORLD, FAR AWAY FROM OUR QUOTIDIAN CONCERNS. CIRQUE'S ARTISTS CREATE WORLDS OF DREAMS AND NIGHT-MARES THAT REFLECT OUR HOPES, FEARS, AND ASPIRATIONS. BUT ONCE THEY STEP OFFSTAGE, WHERE DO THEY GO?

WHAT IS LIFE OUTSIDE THE GRAND CHAPITEAU LIKE FOR THEM?

14/

Every touring Cirque du Soleil show premieres to a hometown audience in Montreal. In the weeks and months before the premiere, artists are cast from around the world and gather in Montreal for rehearsals. Each traveling show employs at least 150 artists, technicians, and support staff full-time. After the initial Montreal run, a new show will typically play in Quebec City and then Toronto before heading for points abroad.

Raising the Grand Chapiteau in a new town is an event treated with ceremony. Big-top raising is a specialized skill, overseen by a tent master. (Qualified tent masters, it appears, are in increasingly short supply and are among the hardest-sought Cirque employees.)

At each stop along the tour, one hundred local people or so are hired as temporary staff, for such things as security, hospitality, and the concession stands.

The show becomes a traveling village where each person's energies are concentrated on the day's performance. Cirque du Soleil does everything it can to create a welcoming, pleasant environment for its artists and technicians, so they can concentrate on putting on the best show possible. Each production travels with a complete kitchen and dining area offering healthy gourmet meals and snacks. Artists and crew are lodged in comfortable hotels or apartments not far from the show site. According to seniority, some are housed in efficiency apartments. Child performers and children of artists are educated in an on-site classroom by teachers instructing them in the standard Quebec school curriculum.

Artists will usually arrive for the evening's performance somewhere in the mid- to late afternoon. Every show is videotaped by coaches who review performances with the artists on a daily basis. Artists and coaches will then work on routines until show time, improving them where they can. Artists undergo physiotherapy when necessary in traveling physiotherapy units. Pre-show time is also filled with consultation with stage managers, a traveling costume department, and the show's artistic director, all with an eye to maximizing performance.

On some shows, workshops with choreographers, acting coaches, or other performance specialists are organized for artists interested in improving their skills. When time permits, artists sit at computer screens, exchanging e-mail with faraway friends and family. Because their schedules from arrival to show time are so full, many artists apply their makeup well before the opening call, to ensure they're ready. As showtime approaches, musicians gather for a daily sound-check. While they play, Trapeze and Bungee artists often swing overhead, practicing their routines to an empty house.

Most pre-show activity is centered in the Artistic Tent, which is connected by a short corridor to the Main Tent. During the show, artists gather around a backstage monitor and follow the action of the show, waiting for their cues.

After the show, some artists and crew gather at the hotel to relax into the early hours. There can be up to ten shows a week, six days a week. On days off, the cast and crew still spend time together, perhaps touring the attractions of the city they're currently stopped in. There can be up to two weeks off between tour stops, during which the cast can catch up with family and friends (while the crew remains busy taking down the Grand Chapiteau and then setting it up in the next town). Some call Montreal home between stops, while others maintain homes in places as diverse as Seattle or Moscow.

In many ways, it's a comfortable, insular existence. As one would expect, close relationships are formed, broken, and formed again. Families come together, and children are born. Some adapt well to the singular lifestyle, others begin to long for a more settled life.

MARC SOHIER AND LINDA BÉLANGER

Marc Sohier has been the bandleader and bass player for *Saltimbanco* since 1994. His partner, Linda Bélanger, has performed as an acrobat with Cirque since 1992. Having met at Cirque du Soleil, they are expecting their first child in 2004, and find that their evolving relationship may ultimately pull them away from life on the road.

"After nine years on the road, you start to need walls around you," explains Sohier. "Linda is pregnant now. We've somehow managed to make a life together on tour. In fact, if I'm still here, it's because of her." The two have planned the delivery of their child around their touring schedule. "The child is due while we're in Zurich," says Bélanger. "Every month or two, I've got to see a doctor wherever we are, a different doctor every time. But we've been lucky. We've visited birthing clinics in Zurich already. We know where we'll be."

When the child is born, both Sohier and Bélanger doubt it will grow up on the road. "Whether you like it or not, what we're living isn't life," Sohier says. "It's a kind of life, but it's not a rooted life, a normal life. It's life in fast-forward: shows every night, people applauding you. It's a kind of dream. Meanwhile, time passes, and you get older."

THE VINTILOV FAMILY

For the acrobatic Vintilov family—Andriy and Oxana, and their children Darya and Maxsim—performing and traveling together appears natural, and bonding.

At first, Andriy and Oxana performed the lyrical Adagio Act in *Saltimbanco* with their daughter, Darya. Their son, Maxsim, five years younger than Darya, grew up watching his family perform together. "When he was very small," Oxana says, "I remember Maxsim asking, 'Mama, why is everyone working except me?'" Her husband joins in: "We said, don't worry, you're going to work.'"

Darya eventually grew too big to continue in the act, and was replaced by Maxsim. "She's my size now," says Oxana, "she grew fast!" Her family on tour with *Saltimbanco*, Darya moved to Montreal for trapeze training. "This is the first time I've spent so much time away from my family," she says of the experience. "At first it was very hard, because I didn't know what to do, I was shocked. I missed traveling. Sometimes it's boring staying in the same place, until you make friends. But, little by little, I've made friends, so it's fine now." After her training, Darya will return to *Saltimbanco* to perform the Solo Trapeze Act, and the traveling Vintilov family will be reunited.

13/
CHILDREN ARE PART OF EVERY TOURING
CIRQUE SHOW. CHILD ARTISTS AND
CHILDREN OF ARTISTS ARE TAUGHT IN
TRAVELING CLASSROOMS, ON SITE.

14/
CLOCKWISE FROM LEFT: ÉRIC ALAIN,
GENNADY CHIZHOV, DMITRI BELIAIKOV.
BACKSTAGE LIFE ON TOUR.
FOR PRACTICAL REASONS, ARTISTS APPLY
MAKEUP AN HOUR OR MORE BEFORE
THE SHOW.

15/
THE VINTILOV FAMILY: ANDRIY VINTILOV,
OXANA VINTILOVA, AND MAXSIM
VINTILOV, ON AND OFF STAGE.

15/

CHAPTER
12

"O"

CREATING A MASTERPIECE

> BEHOLD THIS WORLD, A STAGE
> UPON WHICH WE STRUT, PLAY
> AND DREAM OF BEAUTY
> UNTIL THE FINAL CURTAIN FALLS,
> UNTIL THE FINAL HOUR CALLS.

"O" PREMIERED IN 1998 IN A SPECIALLY CONSTRUCTED THEATER AT THE BELLAGIO HOTEL AND CASINO, ADDING ANOTHER RESIDENT LAS VEGAS SHOW TO THE CIRQUE DU SOLEIL REPERTOIRE. "O" IS A TECHNICAL AND ARTISTIC TRIUMPH, A STUNNING AND INNOVATIVE COMBINATION OF THEATER, AQUATICS, AND ACROBATICS.

BACKED ONCE AGAIN BY STEVE WYNN, THE SHOW WOULD BE AN ENORMOUS, SPECTACULAR UNDERTAKING. FROM THE BEGINNING, FRANCO DRAGONE FELT THAT "O" HAD TO BE A MASTERPIECE.

"WHILE WE WERE PREPARING "O", AT ONE OF THE FIRST MEETINGS WE HAD IN LAS VEGAS I SAID THAT WE ABSOLUTELY HAD TO CREATE A CLASSIC, WE COULDN'T GET AWAY FROM IT," HE RECALLS. "IT WAS THAT, OR NOTHING, BECAUSE OF THE ENORMOUS COST IN ENERGY THAT PEOPLE WOULD BE PUTTING INTO IT. I WANTED "O" TO BE ABOVE CRITICISM. I WANTED "O" TO BE BIGGER THAN WE WERE."

TURNING SPECTACLE INTO THEATER

Guy Laliberté remembers that the original thinking behind "O" was to create spectacle on a monumental scale. "At the first meeting," Laliberté recalls, "there were forty people around the table. Steve Wynn wanted to do something in a pool that would be four times the size of a football field, with water skis, ski jumps, fountains, stunt people ..."

Cirque's first impulse was to turn the spectacular into something more artistic and intimate. "We saw all that," says Laliberté, "and said, 'No, let's do theater instead.'"

"For me, the main theme of "O" was the theater," remembers Franco Dragone, "this place where man invents himself to understand his history, to understand life, to understand the universe. Theater is a machine to understand the universe."

"'O' means something bigger than one person, Dragone says. "O" is inaccessible. "O" is the memory of the theater, a memory where you see a young man plunge into a theater scene, and, all of a sudden, the ghosts of all these characters who inhabited the theater appear. They were once brought to life on the stage, and now they've been woken up by the presence of this young man, for an hour and a half."

03/

"O" MEANS SOMETHING BIGGER THAN ONE PERSON. "O" IS INACCESSIBLE.

Dominique Lemieux remembers plunging headlong into the theatrical theme. "We were really using the theater. We weren't shy about it anymore," she remembers. "With the costumes, the characters, they're very theatrical characters."

In terms of set design, Michel Crête saw "O" as an opportunity to blend the acrobatic elements of a Cirque du Soleil show even more seamlessly into a theatrical environment. "More and more, we wanted to get away from specific acrobatic equipment on stage," he says, "so that artists could perform acrobatics on other structures, structures that were part of the theatrical environment."

Their ultimate goal, as always, was to involve the audience. "We felt that if you could see artists performing on, say, a boat, it would stimulate your imagination more than if you saw them performing on, say, a trapeze."

TAMING WATER

While its intended scope was pared down to fit the theater, "O" nonetheless is a remarkable technical achievement. "We had to learn how to work with water," recalls Guy Laliberté, "an element that by its very nature is not compatible with show business. That's an achievement—you have to remember that we pitched the project at the time of the *Waterworld* fiasco." (*Waterworld*, a science-fiction film set in a watery future, tanked at the box office.)

Laliberté remembers that the key to working with water was letting it dictate its own terms. "Your first reflex is to go against the rhythm of water. But by listening, you come to realize that water wants you to work at its rhythm. That realization helped us come up with something wholly original—it was a creative stimulus of the first order."

Seeking inspiration, Dominique Lemieux visited the watery city of Venice. While there, she saw how water, with its particular romantic rhythm, could be associated with the cycles of life. "I went to Venice and wrote a lot," she says, "and, for me, "O" became about love, the relationship between two people, marriage. All the stages follow one after another, everything we live from birth to death. "O" is about splendor, the splendor of birth." From there, Dominique Lemieux remembers that the watery world of "O" became an oasis, visited by fantastic creatures. "With "O,"" she says, "it's like we took the garden that was *Mystère* and made it bigger. It's like we entered a forest and went further in."

04/

o6/o7/o8/
"O" DREW ITS INSPIRATION FROM WATER.
THE PRODUCTION WAS SHAPED
BY THE CHALLENGE OF WORKING WITH
AN UNPREDICTABLE, POTENTIALLY
DANGEROUS ELEMENT.

o6/

o7/

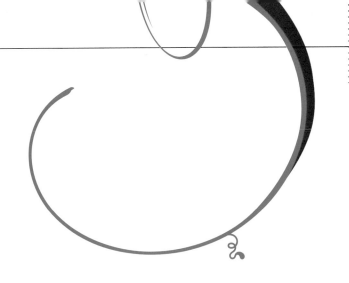

o8/

09/

09/
THE SPECTRAL EUGEN (EUGEN BRIM).

10/

11/
MIKE BROWN, THE FIRE ACT. ORIGINAL PLANS FOR **"O"** CALLED FOR A SHOW BASED ON BOTH WATER AND FIRE. FIRE STILL APPEARS IN THE FINISHED PRODUCTION.

12/
RAY WOLD BURNS NONCHALANTLY.

"WE HAD TO LEARN HOW TO WORK WITH WATER, AN ELEMENT THAT BY ITS VERY NATURE IS NOT COMPATIBLE WITH SHOW BUSINESS."

TECHNICAL CHALLENGES

As well as providing creative stimulus, working with water posed a number of technical challenges. For example, extensive research had to be carried out to see what the stage itself would be made of. The technical crew had to find flooring that could stand up to the strain of constant acrobatic performance and dry off quickly. The costume department had to make the show's wardrobe out of material comfortable and resistant enough for gymnasts and performers to work in that could also stand up the being wet all the time. According to makeup designer Nathalie Gagné,""O" was a huge challenge for the makeup department, not just because of the water, but also because of the bromine and chlorine in it. We tested a lot of things on the synchronized swimmers during rehearsals. Sometimes you'd find something that would stay on in the water, but then couldn't resist the constant getting in and out of the water. We finally found something, but it took a lot of work."

PERFORMING "O"

Despite the challenges, "O" came together easily. Franco Dragone attributes this to the fact that the same core team had worked on so many shows together. "It's not easy to build a team, and the chemistry that exists between people," he points out. "But we developed an organic way of working together. You can really see it in "O". For me, "O" was the synthesis of my work. It's a homage to how people can live and work together."

However, some of the artists in the show found the challenge of working on the show's majestic stage daunting at first. Anja Wyttenbach, who plays the unicycle-riding Aurora and performs the Washington Trapeze Act in the show, remembers an early rehearsal. "Franco gave us a forty-five-minute presentation about the stage and the lifts, and I thought, 'We can't perform on there, it's too beautiful. It's so big, it's going to make us look small.'"

Nathalie Bollinger, a member of the house troupe, says: "This is a very complicated show, with I don't know how many technical cues. I thought, for sure, with water, fire, and electricity, there would be problems technically."

Terry Bartlett, a gymnast turned artist, remembers feeling leery about working in water. "I wasn't sure how much I'd enjoy a water show," he says, "landing in water, being cold, drying off . . . you're not sure whether it's your cup of tea."

Yet each of them, in his or her own way, points to the water as the reason they overcame their initial misgivings. "I think the show is successful because of how the water is integrated," says Wyttenbach. "It's beautiful." As an acrobat, Nathalie Bollinger says, "'O' is easier on your body. It's much better to land in water." Bartlett, who, at thirty-nine, adds that water is especially forgiving for older gymnasts, echoes her sentiments: "'O' is less impact for the body, so at this time of my life, it's better."

14/

RAISING THE BAR

Putting "O" together wasn't always easy. "There were times," notes Guy Laliberté, "when Steve Wynn was scared. We had to work against an attitude that the technical challenges were too big, that we were crazy." In the end, however, "O" became a show that set a new standard in live entertainment. Terry Bartlett speaks of that success with pride. "Cirque is changing the whole world of entertainment. Now, I think people expect shows to be as brilliant, as fantastic, and as good as "O." We've laid down the gauntlet." Guy Laliberté puts it even more succinctly: "With "O," we guaranteed ourselves a page in the history of the theater."

14/
THE DUO TRAPEZE ACT, PERFORMED BY ALIFIA AND ZULFIA ALIMOVA.

15/
ENKHEE TUMENDELGER SWIMS WEARING MAKEUP SPECIALLY DESIGNED TO WITH-STAND PERFORMANCE IN WATER.

16/
BARGE, LIKE SO MUCH IN "O," IS PART ACT, PART TABLEAU.

17/
WHITE PIERROT, SKETCHED BY DOMINIQUE LEMIEUX: THE CHARACTER NEVER APPEARED IN THE SHOW.

17/

18/

18/
LA PARADE

A WATERY REFLECTION

Whatever its technical and artistic achievements, it could be that "O" is acclaimed because, like all Cirque shows, audiences find something of themselves in it. While we marvel at its achievements, "O" draws us into our own hopes and fears.

"You can watch this show and come back to see it again and again, and each time you'll see something different," says Terry Bartlett. "Because your life has changed, and our lives have changed."

19/

MAKEUP:

BEAUTY IN CLOSE-UP

21/
Carlos Márcio Moreira, *La Nouba*.

22/
Gareth Hopkins, *Varekai*.

23/
Nathalie Gagné, Makeup Designer,
with Raquel Karro, *Varekai*.

24/
Sandra Feusi, *Saltimbanco*.

25/
Tools of the trade. Artists use these
to apply their own makeup.

26/
Stella Umeh, *Varekai*.

27/
Gareth Hopkins, *Varekai*.

28/
Andrew Atherton, *Varekai*.

PART OF THE BEAUTY OF "O" OR OF ANY CIRQUE DU SOLEIL SHOW, IS THE MAKEUP WORN BY ITS CHARACTERS. AS MUCH AS THE COSTUMES OR SET DESIGN, MAKEUP IS AN INTEGRAL AND UNMISTAKABLE PART OF CIRQUE'S VISUAL SIGNATURE.

NATHALIE GAGNÉ HAS BEEN THE PRINCIPAL MAKEUP DESIGNER ON EIGHT CIRQUE DU SOLEIL SHOWS SO FAR. IN EACH SHOW, THE MAKEUP FOR INDIVIDUAL CHARACTERS IS INSPIRED BY SKETCHES FROM THE COSTUME DESIGNER, AND THEN DEVELOPED BY THE MAKEUP DESIGNER AND COSTUME DESIGNER TOGETHER.

Individual performers are then required to apply their own makeup.

Carolyne Vita, a performer in *Saltimbanco*, describes the process this way. "They create your character's makeup. Then, during training in Montreal, they try it out on you. If it works, the makeup designer then provides a step-by-step sheet so you can do it yourself and practices with you as much as time allows, to get it right.

"It's essentially a cream-based makeup that you have to neutralize with a powder, so it doesn't smear. Then you paint on top of it with a colored powder and water-based eyeliner or mascara.

"The girls in the costume shop always double-check us before the show, to make sure it's right."

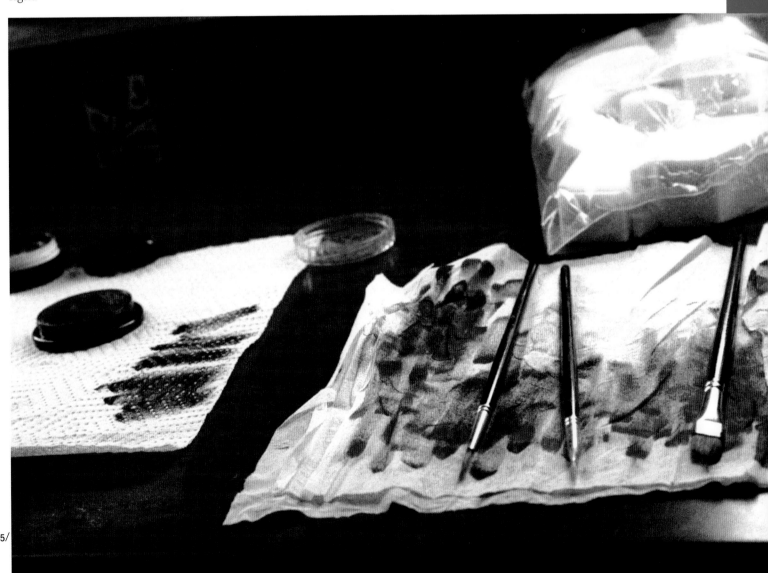

27/

28/

LA NOUBA

FAIRY TALES IN THE ATTIC

> ONCE UPON A TIME,
> IN AN ATTIC OF THE MIND
> DREAMS AND NIGHTMARES CAME TO LIFE
> AND TOLD A STORY OF LAUGHTER,
> HOPE, AND TEARS.
> ONCE UPON A TIME IS NOW.

SOON AFTER "O"'s TRIUMPH IN LAS VEGAS, CIRQUE DU SOLEIL PREMIERED *LA NOUBA*, ANOTHER PERMANENT SHOW. LIKE *MYSTÈRE* AND "O," *LA NOUBA* IS PRESENTED IN A SPECIALLY CONSTRUCTED THEATER. UNLIKE EITHER, *LA NOUBA*'S THEATER IS A FREE-STANDING, INDEPENDENT STRUCTURE AT WALT DISNEY WORLD RESORTS, IN ORLANDO, FLORIDA.

FOR CIRQUE AND DISNEY, *LA NOUBA* WAS THE FRUIT OF TEN YEARS OF NEGOTIATION, AND THE FULFILLMENT OF LONG-STANDING AMBITION ON THE PART OF DISNEY TO INCLUDE CIRQUE DU SOLEIL IN ITS ROSTER.

DISNEY HEAD MICHAEL EISNER REMEMBERS THAT NEGOTIATIONS WITH CIRQUE DU SOLEIL WERE LONG AND COMPLEX, BECAUSE CIRQUE INSISTED ON RETAINING CREATIVE INDEPENDENCE. HIS SOLUTION WAS TO LET CIRQUE HAVE IT. "I'VE BEEN DEALING WITH THE MOVIE BUSINESS FOR A LONG TIME," SAYS EISNER IN THE DOCUMENTARY *RUN BEFORE YOU FLY*, "AND WHEN YOU HAVE A SPIELBERG OR A GEORGE LUCAS OR OTHERS OF THAT LEVEL, YOU LET THEM HAVE CREATIVE CONTROL. WITH CIRQUE DU SOLEIL AND GUY LALIBERTÉ, YOU CREATE A FINANCIAL BOX, AND YOU LET THEM DO IT."

A FAIRY TALE, CIRQUE-STYLE

Looking back on *La Nouba*, Guy Laliberté remembers: "Being at the heart of Disney, the master of the fairy tale, necessarily meant that we had to tell a fairy tale in our own way."

Michel Crête remembers the idea of fairy tales directly influencing the design and conception of the *La Nouba* theater and stage. "We were at Disney, so we were influenced by the world of fables," he says. "Plus, the performance space was our first stand-alone building, so we had to deal with that. We saw the structure as a kind of castle from a fairy tale. The set is like an attic where we tell each other fairy tales."

01/
JULIA PARROT PERFORMS
THE AERIAL BALLET IN SILK.

02/
THE NUTS, PLAYED, FROM LEFT TO RIGHT,
BY JUSTIN OSBOURNE, PAVEL BIEGAJ,
DAVID LEBEL, AND WITEK BIEGAJ—
EMBODY *LA NOUBA*'S ANARCHIC SPIRIT.

03/
SKETCHES BY DOMINIQUE LEMIEUX.

04/
THE GREEN BIRD, PLAYED BY ELENA DAY.

03/

"BEING AT THE HEART OF DISNEY, THE MASTER OF THE FAIRY TALE, NECESSARILY MEANT THAT WE HAD TO TELL A FAIRY TALE IN OUR OWN WAY."

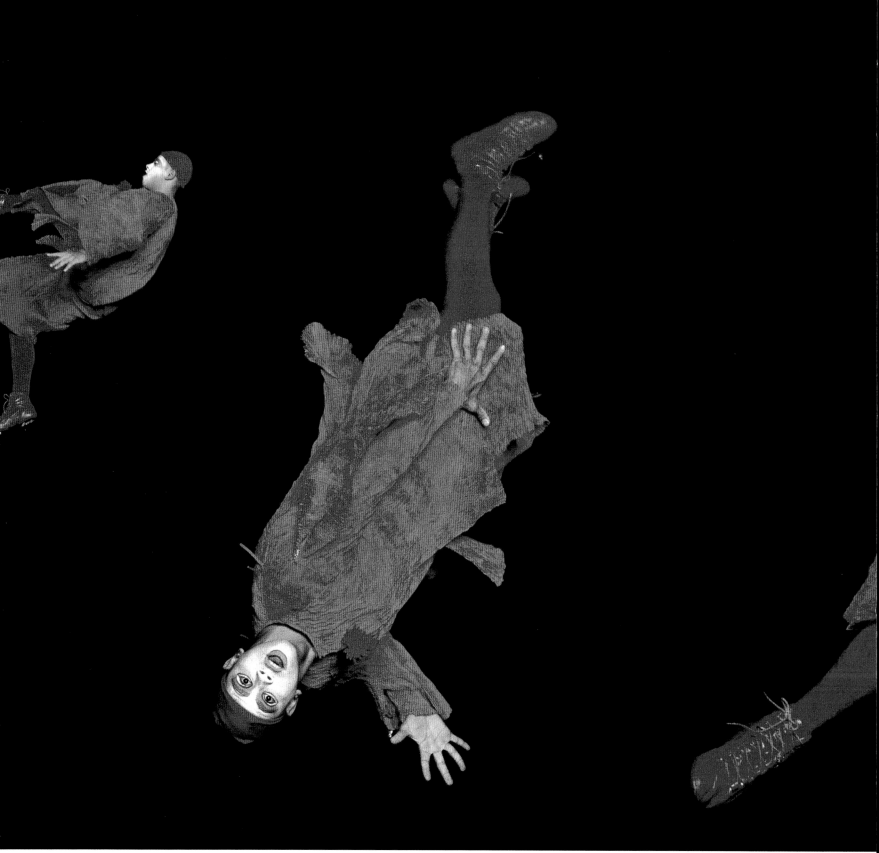

"THAT HAPPINESS YOU SEE IN THE YOUNG PERFORMERS IS A HYMN TO JOY!"

07/

TURNING EXHAUSTION INTO ENERGY

Every member of the creative team remembers coming to *La Nouba* feeling depleted after working straight through a challenging string of previous shows. *Mystère, Alegría, Quidam,* and "O" had all been overlapping productions. Somehow, Cirque had also found time to put together a film production inspired by *Alegría* in the same period. The group's fatigue when they came to *La Nouba* was compounded by the fact that there was very little time to put the show together.

Their collective response was to plumb the energy of youth, long the motor of Cirque du Soleil's inventive power.

La Nouba "was made under exhaustion," admits Laliberté. "What helped us get through it," he continues, "was to make the show a tribute to all the teenagers in the world, which injected a lot of energy into it."

The result is a show that radiates youth. "*La Nouba* has something close to *Saltimbanco* in it," reflects Dominique Lemieux. "It's very young. The casting is very young. There's a freshness and a simplicity to the show. There wasn't much time to do it. I drew and produced the costumes in three months! It was a frenzy. But it gave the show something light, fun, and relevant."

For Laliberté, that energy is especially apparent in the show's finale. "That act is a masterpiece," he says. "That happiness you see in the young performers is a hymn to joy!"

08/

10/

09/

12/

13/
RED PIERROT (WELLINGTON LIMA).

14/
LA NOUBA'S CLIMACTIC POWER
TRACK/TRAMPOLINE ACT.

13/

A HIP-HOP SHOW

Franco Dragone gave the youthful energy of the show a funkier
edge, inspired by a desire to please his teenage son. "I wanted to
prove to my son that I could do a hip-hop show," he remembers.

The result is a show with a unique visual signature,
according to lighting designer Luc Lafortune, who has worked
on every Cirque show so far. "I wanted a modern urban feel," says
Lafortune. "That's why you see 'shift,' 'delete' and bar codes on the
walls. It's a show with a high-tech feel, in the style of *Metropolis*."

FAREWELL FOR NOW?

For the creative team behind so many of Cirque's shows in the
1990s, *La Nouba* was the conclusion of a remarkable run of artistic and professional achievement. Franco Dragone, Michel Crête,
and Dominique Lemieux would leave the creative reins to future
shows in the hands of others.

Their distinctive style of working and creating had been a
major influence not only on Cirque du Soleil's shows but on its
entire corporate culture. Dealing with their absence would
mean a major adjustment as Cirque du Soleil neared the end of
the decade.

15/
The world of *La Nouba*...
Left to right: Carlos Moreira as
The Walker, Justin Osbourne, Pavel
Biegaj, David Lebel and Witek Biegaj
as The Nuts, Wellington Lima
as Red Pierrot, Krystian Sawicki as
Titan, Virginia Imazquijera as the
Cleaning Lady, Elena Day
as Green Bird.

15/

DREAMS IN THE ATTIC:
THE BIRTH OF THE STUDIO

FOR YEARS, CIRQUE DU SOLEIL HAS RECOGNIZED THE IMPORTANCE OF HAVING ITS OWN SPACE TO DREAM AND TELL STORIES IN, LIKE THE ATTIC IN **LA NOUBA**. CIRQUE DU SOLEIL CREATED THAT SPACE IN 1997, WHEN THE MONTREAL STUDIO WAS FOUNDED. SINCE THEN, EVERY CIRQUE EFFORT HAS BEEN CONCEIVED, PRODUCED, COORDINATED, AND SUPPORTED FROM THIS INTERNATIONAL HEADQUARTERS.

16/

AN INTERNATIONAL CENTER FOR CREATIVITY

Guy Laliberté's vision for the Studio is simple: "We wanted to create an international center for creativity. We hope that creators from around the world will want to come and work here."

As of 2004, the Studio welcomes close to three thousand employees and artists from forty countries, speaking twenty-five different languages. It houses three state-of-the-art training studios, as well as an atelier devoted to technical experimentation and development.

Cirque established the Studio in Montreal's Saint-Michel district, one of the poorest areas in North America, in an effort to revitalize the neighborhood and give something back to the community. The Studio features regular art exhibitions and performances, in an effort to integrate the arts into the daily lives of its employees and the community.

INVALUABLE SUPPORT

The Montreal Studio is also home to a large part of Cirque's staff of 3,000. Cirque du Soleil's shows would be impossible without their dedication. These artisans include accountants, acrobats, acupuncturists, aquatics specialists, administrators, architects, archivists, artist support personnel, automation specialists, auxiliary resource personnel, babysitters, backstage technicians, box office personnel, building service technicians, butlers, buyers, cameramen and camerawomen, carpenters, cashiers, clerks, clowns, coaches, comedians, community relations personnel, composers, cooks, costume designers and technicians, cultural agents, customer service personnel, customs advisors, dishwashers, documentation supervisors, draftspersons, drivers, electricians, electro-mechanic technicians, estimators, fabric designers, finance personnel, fly-ins, food and beverage personnel, gardeners, graphic designers, hair dressers, purchasing agents, hospitality personnel, housing personnel, human resources personnel, infrastructure specialists, internal communication personnel, international cooperation personnel, interpreters, IT personnel, jugglers, lace-makers, law personnel, licensing agents, lighting technicians, logistical personnel, maintenance personnel, marketing specialists, merchandising specialists, milliners, musicians, painters, payroll specialists, pilots, production personnel, projectionists, prop masters, prototypists, public affairs agents, public relations agents, public sales personnel, public service workers, publicists, purchasing agents, quality control experts, R&D specialists, receptionists, researchers, retail supervisors, revisers, rigging experts, runners, scouts, secretaries, security guards, shoemakers, construction personnel, social affairs personnel, sound specialists, special effects personnel, stage managers, teachers, tent masters, therapists, tour managers, traffic agents, translators, travel coordinators, treasurers, ushers, videographers, wardrobe specialists, warehouse personnel, welders, and wigmakers, to name just a few.

There are also offices in Orlando, Las Vegas, Amsterdam, and Melbourne, which report to Montreal. "Cirque isn't just the people you see at our shows, as important as they are," says Laliberté. "It's also all the people you don't see providing administrative support. The Studio serves as their headquarters in Montreal, and is a place where they can mingle with the artists and creators on a day-to-day basis."

THE COSTUME WORKSHOP: GROWING EVER-LARGER

Perhaps the most distinguishing feature of the Studio is its Costume Workshop, the only one of its kind in North America. Each Cirque du Soleil costume is custom-made, and constructed from beginning to end at the shop, which covers a total area of 4,180 square meters, and employs specialists in shoemaking, textile design, lace-making, wig-making, millinery, and more.

In 2003, the Costume Shop produced more than 15,500 pieces. Since 1998, it has constructed and modified more than four thousand pairs of shoes.

As Cirque grows, so does the Costume Workshop, a fact that hasn't escaped its principal costume designer. "The fact that Cirque has become so big is overwhelming," comments Dominique Lemieux. "I mean, the [costume] department can't get any bigger, or we'd have to move around on skateboards or Rollerblades!"

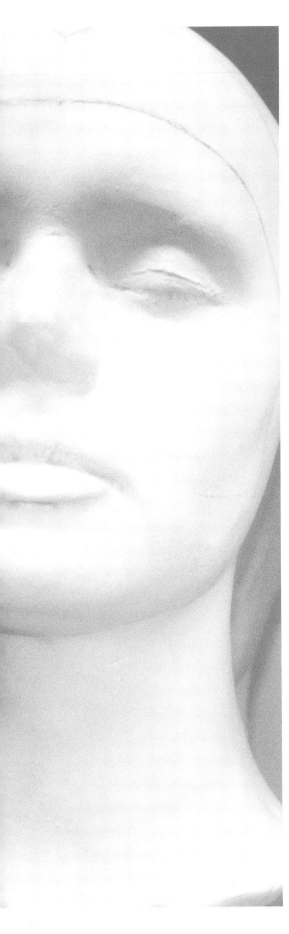

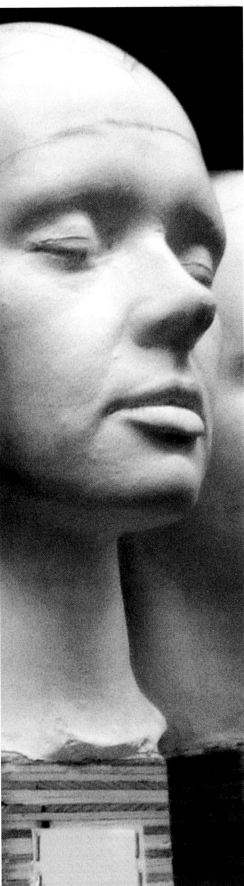

16/
THE MONTREAL STUDIO.

17/
THE MONTREAL STUDIO CONTAINS THREE STATE-OF-THE-ART TRAINING WORKSHOPS.

18/
STONE ARCHWAY BY SCOTTISH ARTIST ANDY GOLDSWORTHY. ONE OF THE MANY WORKS OF ART ON DISPLAY AT CIRQUE'S MONTREAL HEADQUARTERS.

19/20/
COSTUMES FOR EACH CIRQUE SHOW ARE MANUFACTURED AT THE STUDIO. CASTS ARE MADE OF EACH ARTIST'S HEAD AND KEPT IN THE COSTUME WORKSHOP WHEN NEW, INDIVIDUALLY FITTED HEADPIECES ARE REQUIRED.

23/
THE CASTS ARE MADE BY APPLYING PLASTER TO THE ARTISTS' HEADS. THEY MUST KEEP THEIR EYES CLOSED AND BREATHE THROUGH NOSE TUBES WHILE THE PLASTER DRIES.

CHAPTER
14

DRALION
CULTURES COLLIDE

**► EARTH, AIR, FIRE, AND WATER
TAKE ON HUMAN FORM
IN A WORLD WITHOUT TIME
WHERE MAGIC HOLDS SWAY.
CULTURES COLLIDE,
MAN AND NATURE BECOME ONE
AND HARMONY RULES AGAIN.**

DRALION, WHICH PREMIERED IN 1999, REPRESENTED A TRUE CLASH OF CULTURES. IT WAS THE FIRST SHOW IN CIRQUE'S HISTORY TO COMBINE CIRQUE DU SOLEIL'S STYLE WITH THE CHINESE CIRCUS TRADITION ON A LARGE SCALE. BECAUSE IT WAS THE FIRST SHOW TO BE MADE WITHOUT THE CREATIVE GUIDANCE OF FRANCO DRAGONE AND HIS TEAM IN YEARS, IT ALSO REPRESENTED A MAJOR SHIFT IN CIRQUE'S INTERNAL CULTURE.

DESPITE THIS—OR PERHAPS BECAUSE OF IT—*DRALION* HAS RECEIVED ENTHUSIASTIC PUBLIC RESPONSE. TODAY, IT IS A POTENT SYMBOL OF HOW DIFFERENCES CAN BE RESPECTED AND OVERCOME.

AN UNEASY GENESIS

The development of *Dralion* was difficult from the start. Several months into preproduction on the new show, the French director slated for the project abandoned ship. "I was one of the first people to work on *Dralion*, which was called *Cirque 1999* at the time," remembers Sylvie Galarneau, who would become artistic director of the show. "I went to work in Paris with a French director who was first chosen to work on the project. We worked with him for a year, and, after that, he freaked out. He said the project was too big and he couldn't be comfortable working in that environment. Culturally, he was very different."

Faced with the challenge of mounting a new show, with a new team, in a compressed period of time, Guy Laliberté turned to an old friend: Guy Caron.

02/

AN OLD FRIEND RETURNS

For Laliberté, *Dralion* was "an opportunity to reconnect with an old friend, and bring him back into the fold." *Dralion* would mark Guy Caron's return to Cirque after a long absence.

Since he had left Cirque in 1988, Caron had maintained friendly relations with Laliberté. In 1992, he had even directed a show called *Cirque Knie Presents Cirque du Soleil* for the Swiss National Circus, produced in close collaboration with Cirque.

Caron's job wasn't easy: to build a new show, with a creative team largely new to Cirque that would have to meet very high expectations indeed. Together, Caron and Laliberté turned that challenge into an opportunity to fulfill a long-standing goal.

"There was a big dream behind Dralion," explains Laliberté. "Guy Caron and I had visited the Orient in 1986, and from that moment on we dreamed of working with the Chinese, with their incredibly high level of acrobatic skills."

BACK TO BASICS

Faced with a tight deadline, and with the realities of working with the Chinese, Laliberté and Caron were not able to work in the intuitive, workshopping style championed by Dragone and company. "We thought the Chinese would be ready to jump into the creative laboratory," recollects Laliberté, "but we had to approach the mise-en-scène from a completely different angle."

Caron remembers being up for the challenge. "When I came back to direct *Dralion*, I said 'This is who I am, take it or leave it.' My show is totally different from "O", *La Nouba* or Cirque's other shows. To start with, we were working with Chinese artists. At the time, they were more limited in what they could do." While the Chinese performers certainly were not limited in the acrobatic sense, Caron quickly understood that, as ultra-disciplined artists of the communist system and members of the Red Army, they would not adapt easily to the free-form workshopping methods established by Dragone. So, rather than attempt a Dragone-style show, he revisited the earlier style of *Le Cirque réinventé*.

"I like a show that's full of energy, without gaps, that's full of strong acts, funny, with a big punch at the end," Caron says. "That's the vision that I had when I brought Franco in years ago, and it's the vision I still have."

"We said, 'Okay, we'll forget all about the characters and some of the other things that Franco did," continues Caron. "Instead, I opted to explore the root of the circus, and to adhere to a very high technical standard. I also wanted to mix the Cirque du Soleil style with the Chinese style. Plus, I wanted to make the funniest show we could."

Describing the result, Caron adds, "For me, when the little boy runs onstage and starts the clock, he's setting a whole mini-universe in motion: a universe that's funny, where human limitations are constantly surpassed."

04/

"WHEN THE LITTLE BOY RUNS ONSTAGE AND STARTS THE CLOCK, HE'S SETTING A WHOLE MINI-UNIVERSE IN MOTION: A UNIVERSE THAT'S FUNNY, WHERE HUMAN LIMITATIONS ARE CONSTANTLY SURPASSED."

05/

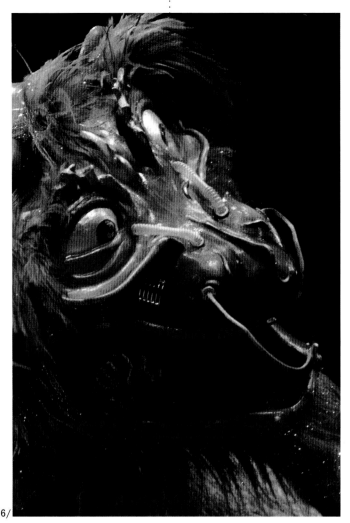

06/

07/

NEW CREATIVE VOICES

Almost all of the players on *Dralion*'s creative team with Caron were new to Cirque du Soleil. These included set designer Stéphane Roy (no relation to Serge Roy), who had been part of the Balcon Vert Youth Hostel crowd in Baie-Saint-Paul so many years before. François Barbeau, a veteran of the Quebec theater scene, designed the costumes. Violaine Corradi, who scored the show, had been active in theater before joining Cirque.

Corradi describes the process of picking up on a preexisting culture and tradition as a delicate one. "I admired what René Dupéré and Benoit Jutras had done," she says, "but, as I saw it, there was a choice I had to make. Do I follow in their footsteps? Or do I do what I like and take that leap of faith and ask, 'What can I bring to the party?'"

Corradi suggests that she was able to find her own voice within Cirque by following the dictates of the show. "One can listen to *Saltimbanco* or *Alegría* and think, 'This is really simple, I can do this,'" she says, "but it's hard! Because you're at the service of a show. What does the director want? What do the artists want? Most importantly, what does Guy Laliberté want? The music has to contribute to this voyage around the world that Cirque wants to take you on."

04/
TEETERBOARD.

06/
LEFT: THE DRALION

07/
RIGHT: AN ARTIST FROM THE HOOP
DIVING ACT LOOKS OUT FROM BACKSTAGE.

08/

"ONSTAGE, SHE SAW PEOPLE FROM DIFFERENT CULTURES WORKING HAND-IN-HAND TO MAKE A SUCCESS OF SOMETHING. IT GAVE HER **HOPE.**"

09/

10/

A ROUGH RIDE

Despite the best efforts of the creative team and the artists to find a new mode of expression, the initial reaction to *Dralion* within Cirque itself was less than generous. For some, according to Sylvie Galarneau, the change from the old order was too much. "Franco had been there with his own style," she recalls, "and even if his shows weren't quite ready when they started, people believed they'd turn out all right. Somehow, what we did was too big a change for a lot of people within Cirque to digest. We thought: 'My God, what have we done?'"

A CELEBRATION OF DIFFERENCE

Despite a rocky start, *Dralion* quickly found its audience and became Cirque du Soleil's top-grossing touring show. The video version of *Dralion* also won a Primetime EMMY Award.

Perhaps the reason for *Dralion*'s success is that Cirque du Soleil is built on celebrating differences. "Even though there are so many Chinese artists in the show, we didn't want it to be perceived as a 'Chinese show,'" explains Violaine Corradi. "But it is an attempt to merge cultures. So, in the hoop number, for instance, I'm doing a very African thing. As far back as 1998, I had this idea of mixing Indian raga with that African beat. So we did it, with Chinese artists jumping all over the place. There's an attempt to bring the audience into a metaphor that we're all One. We come from a Unity, but there's also a Diversity which creates this Unity."

A REASSURING MESSAGE

For Guy Laliberté, *Dralion* "shows how cultural differences can be overcome, and can work together to make something happen. It was hard, but you can see the results."

To drive his point home, Laliberté tells a story about *Dralion* that occurred just after the terrible events of September 11, 2001. "The biggest compliment we could have gotten about the show was two days after 9/11. *Dralion* was in Boston, where the hijacked airplanes had taken off. The producers who had shows going in Boston wondered if they should cancel or not. And all of them said: 'No, it's our responsibility to keep the public entertained.'"

"In the same way, the audiences were wondering if they should go to the shows they had bought tickets for. We received a letter from a woman who was thinking about it for two days before she went. She finally decided: 'Okay, I'll turn off the TV and try to clear my mind by going to see *Dralion*.'"

"At the show, she saw clearly that what the world was going through right then could have a whole other side to it. Onstage, she saw people from different cultures working hand-in-hand to make a success of something. It gave her hope.

"Her letter convinced me that this little dream you have can make a huge impact on people. What gives me the most satisfaction is seeing that impact, that we can change people's lives."

12/

13/

CLOWNS

FROM SHOW TO SHOW, WHATEVER ITS UNDERLYING THEME OR MOOD, CIRQUE DU SOLEIL HAS ALWAYS FEATURED CLOWN ACTS. WITH SOME EXCEPTIONS, THESE ACTS ARE DEVELOPED BY WORLD-CLASS CLOWNS AND CIRCUS PERFORMERS LIKE AMERICAN DAVID SHINER, RUSSIAN SLAVA POLUNIN, CANADIAN RENÉ BAZINET, AND ENGLISHMAN BRIAN DEWHURST.

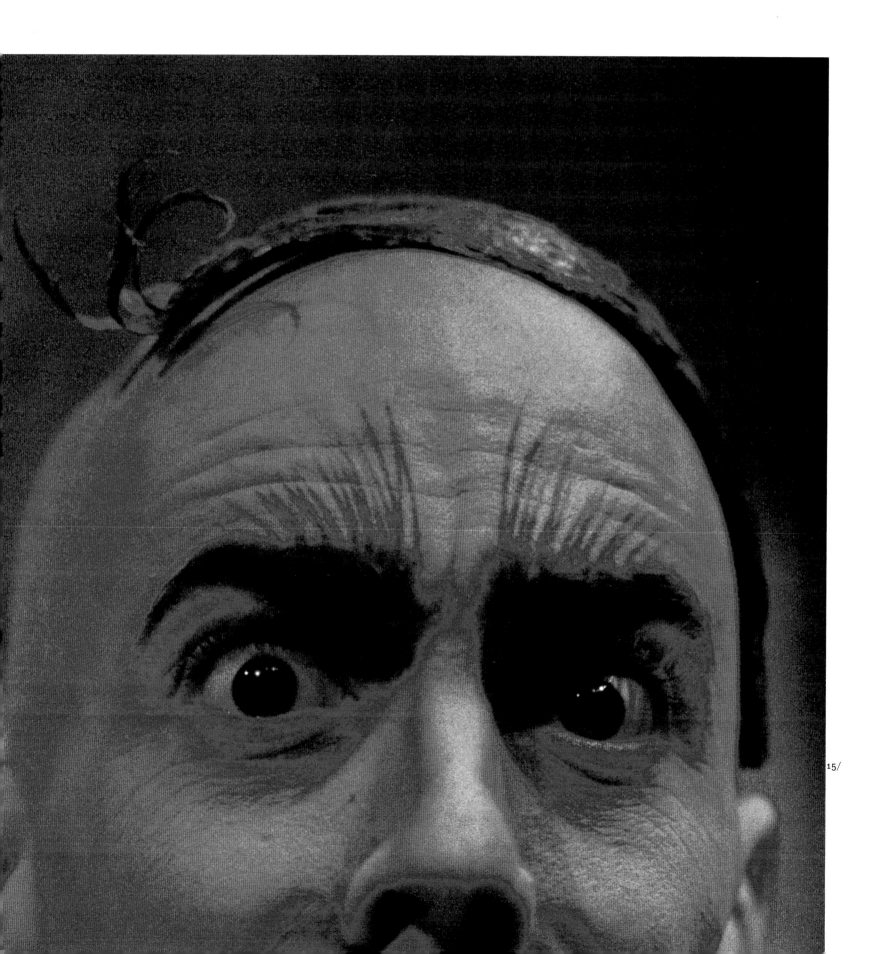

16/

17/

"YOU CAN'T JUST HAVE CIRCUS SKILLS. COMICS BREAK THE TENSION, AND ADD LAUGHTER TO A WHOLE RANGE OF EMOTIONS."

19/

Cirque du Soleil clowns work closely with the creative team to integrate their acts and characters into a specific show. Often, once the performer's run on the show is completed, the character remains, played by a succession of new performers.

"How can you create a circus show without comics?" asks Guy Caron. "You can't just have circus skills. Comics break the tension, and add laughter to a whole range of emotions."

Cirque du Soleil is dedicated to keeping the clown tradition alive. "There's a problem," continues Caron, "the world is actually running out of clowns. There are no schools for clowns. So much comedy today is verbal. The good clowns can teach, but they're usually old. It takes maturity to be a good clown. You have to know who you are to be able to laugh at yourself."

20/

PART 3

STILL SHINING:

2000 – PRESENT DAY

FOR CIRQUE DU SOLEIL, ENTERING A NEW DECADE MEANT COMING FACE TO FACE WITH A DIFFICULT QUESTION. HOW DO YOU STAY TRUE TO YOUR ROOTS WHILE CONTINUING TO MOVE IN NEW DIRECTIONS?

A NEW ORGANIZATION

DANIEL GAUTHIER LEAVES A VOID

On February 2, 2001, a going-away party was held for Daniel Gauthier. Everyone from the early days was there: René Dupéré's old street musician group, La Fanfafonie, even reunited for the occasion. The party was a testament to just how much Gauthier was appreciated within Cirque.

While less known to the public, Gauthier had been a huge presence within Cirque. Nothing happened without his knowledge or approval. Serge Côté, Cirque's in-house Information coordinator, remembers that "Daniel was extremely sharp, a real perfectionist. He read everything, every memo, every contract, every proposal, in detail. And he'd always surprise people with his response—he'd always see something they missed."

While the mood at the party was undoubtedly festive, a sense of doubt hung in the air. How would Cirque manage without his close stewardship? For all its success, could Cirque du Soleil hold it together without him?

The split, according to Laliberté, was without rancor: "At a certain point—I think a good point for both him and Cirque—Daniel made a personal decision to pursue other things. We're still neighbors, we're still friends."

Still, the question must have hung heavily over Cirque's founder. As Côté remembers, "Internally, people were really shaken when Daniel left, and Guy had to reassure them many times over." Gilles Ste-Croix, eager to pursue his own dream of reviving the show-riding tradition, had once again left to produce Cheval, a traveling horse show (Laliberté was a minority partner in the venture). Laliberté was left to face the storm alone.

After its rough-and-tumble beginnings, its first adventures in Japan, and its forays into Las Vegas, Cirque du Soleil had reached a turning point yet again.

Laliberté, barely 40, was a success. He no longer needed to

WHILE ALREADY ENGAGED IN THE PROCESS OF REPLACING HIS CORE CREATIVE TEAM, GUY LALIBERTÉ FACED YET ANOTHER CHALLENGE WHEN DANIEL GAUTHIER, HIS BUSINESS PARTNER SINCE 1987, ANNOUNCED HIS DEPARTURE.

stay with Cirque du Soleil. He could have easily left the company and lived in comfort for the rest of his days. Instead, he decided to remain at the helm and restructure the company's management, promoting Lyn Heward to President & C.O.O., Creative Content Division, and eventually hiring Daniel Lamarre as President and C.O.O., Shows and New Ventures Divisions.

Rather than being the end of Cirque, Laliberté decided, Daniel Gauthier's departure would mark a new chapter. Cirque du Soleil's "Volume 2" had officially begun. "Volume 2," says Laliberté, "will be about establishing Cirque du Soleil's legacy. And we've just started writing it."

The latest stage in Cirque's history has been marked by new creative teams, increasing collaboration with talented artists from outside Cirque, and, as ever, a willingness to embrace the unexpected.

CHAPTER
15

VAREKAI

EMBRACING CHAOS

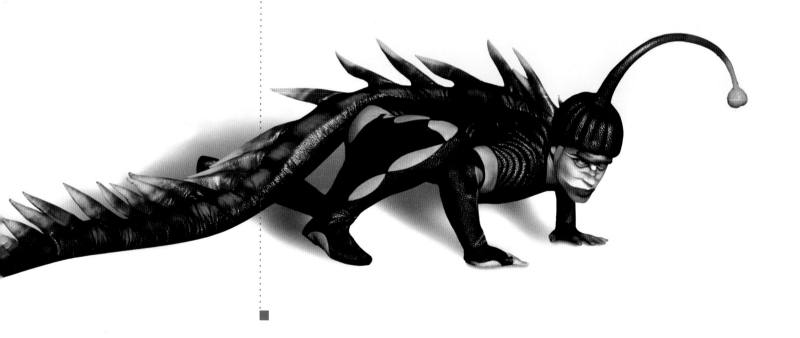

> **LIFE IS SUBJECT TO CHANGE WITHOUT NOTICE. TAKE COMFORT IN CHAOS. THE FOREST MAY BE DARK AND DEEP IN FEAR, BUT EVERY ROAD LEADS THE SEEKER HOME.**

DEALING WITH CHANGE

As the production of *Dralion* had shown, dealing with the absence of Dragone, Crête, and Lemieux on its new shows would be tricky. Guiding the creation of the show while making up for Gauthier's departure would be an additional challenge for Guy Laliberté.

For the company's founder, the proper response to change was to go back to Cirque's roots. "I always said we were a Quebec company," he says now, "and that creativity in Quebec was a natural resource. It made sense to get a director in Quebec." That director turned out to be a young man named Dominic Champagne.

02/

ENTER DOMINIC CHAMPAGNE

Dominic Champagne defines himself as "a writer and a director, a man of the theater." Like his predecessor Franco Dragone, the theater for Champagne means exploring conventional forms, and a heightened relationship with the audience. "I'm not just the kind of theater person who plays with Beckett or Shakespeare," he says. "I try to create my own universes, and I try to find a fusion between music, cabaret, and dramatic performance. I want there to be a party between the performers and the audience. I think it's the spirit of wanting to mix the spectacular and the dramatic that interested Guy, who invited me in."

Laliberté recalls clicking with Champagne quickly. "We looked around, and we met many people," he recalls. "Within five minutes, I felt comfortable with Dominic as a person. I went to see a show he was doing and found it interesting. We shook hands and decided to go for it."

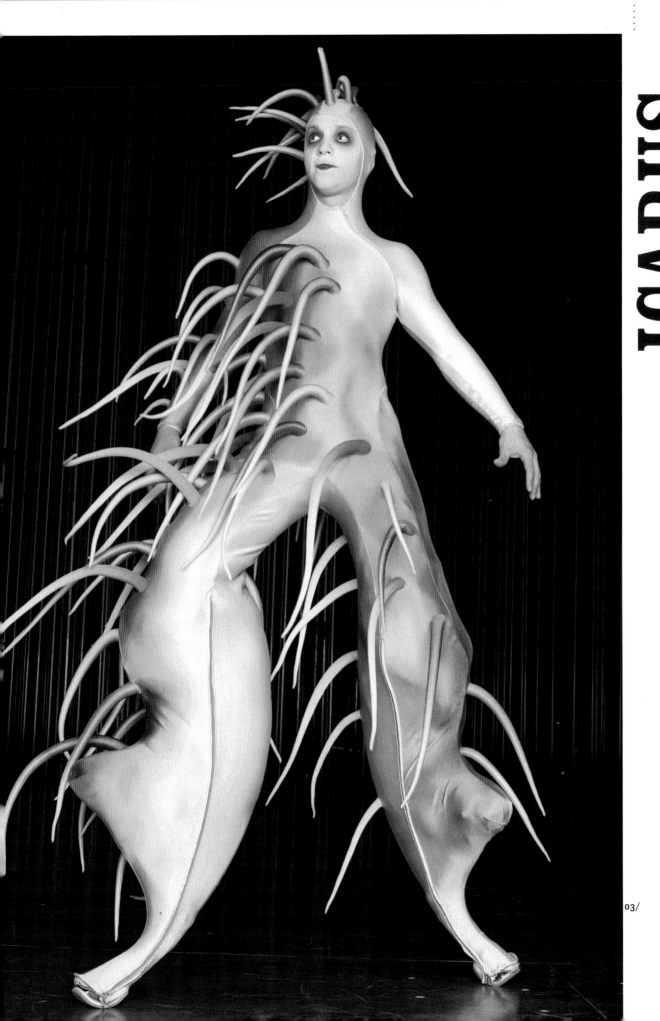

ICARUS.

WE WERE INSPIRED BY THE MYTH OF ICARUS.
THE STORY TAKES UP AFTER THE MYTH ENDS.
WHAT HAPPENED TO ICARUS AFTER HIS FALL?

03/

04/

04/
GEORGIAN DANCE: KHVICHA TETVADZE,
TEMUR KORIDZE, AND BADRI ESATIA.

"WE WANTED TO CONFRONT THE MAIN CHARACTER WITH STRANGERS. WE CONSTANTLY MEET STRANGERS, AND WE EXPE- RIENCE THAT FASCINATION AND FEAR. WE'RE CURIOUS ABOUT THEM, BUT ALSO A LITTLE HOSTILE TOWARD THEM."

DEVELOPING A NEW PROCESS

For Champagne and his new team, many of whom were strangers to one another, the intuitive approach to creation championed by Dragone would be difficult to replicate. As Lyn Heward explains, "The problem with intuitive is that it doesn't necessarily happen spontaneously. It takes time to develop. The original group did eight or ten shows together, and that was over a period of time."

Faced with that reality, Champagne responded by presenting a scripted show. This new "top down" approach represented a true turning point in Cirque's history. "The fact is that every show from *Varekai* on has been written," admits Heward, "in the sense that the director will come in and say, 'Okay, here's my vision of the thing.' Then you're trying, in some way, to match people to that vision."

06/

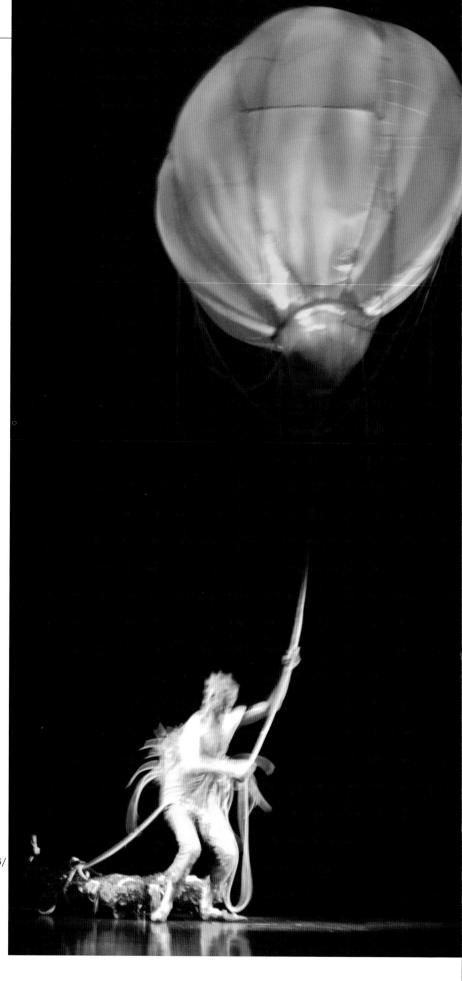

o6/
BUT WILL IT FLY?
JOHN GILKEY AS THE SKYWATCHER.
WITH A NEW CREATIVE TEAM AT THE HELM,
SOME MAY HAVE WONDERED IF *VAREKAI*
WOULD SUCCEED AS WELL AS
PREVIOUS SHOWS.

o7/
KEVIN AND ANDREW ATHERTON PERFORM
THE AERIAL STRAPS ACT.

o7/

08/

09/

TELLING A STORY

From Champagne's perspective, taking a more narrative approach would allow him to breathe fresh air into the Cirque oeuvre. "We weren't trying to make a revolution. The bar is already set high," he remembers. "But I thought that what I could bring to a Cirque show is to try to integrate drama and acrobatics more. In other words, to tell a story, or give a little more meaning to the acrobatic numbers."

Champagne's new approach would allow the new creative team to speak in its own voice. "Franco Dragone, Dominique Lemieux, and Michel Crête established an extremely strong identity, and the only thing I could do is to study it, and see how they worked, to see how they found the solutions they did," he says. "At the same time, I find it hard to be like someone else. You have to be authentic and find your own way into things."

Varekai's narrative line was built in answer to a simple question. "We were inspired by the myth of Icarus," says Champagne. "The story takes up after the myth ends. What happened to Icarus after his fall?

"We have a character in the show who's like a bird with a broken wing. He's in free fall, and he lands in this magic forest where he's going to have to learn to walk again, to fly again, to enter into communion with others.

"The show is built around his journey, and each acrobatic performance is another stage where the main character learns something, so that, ultimately, through a series of small steps, he finds happiness in this world he's fallen into."

"IN VAREKAI, YOU'RE LOOKING AT THIS TRIBE, MAYBE AT ANOTHER LEVEL OF CONSCIOUSNESS, A KIND OF GYPSY CAMP."

10/

11/

12/

13/   14/

WE ARE ALL NOMADS

To create the characters that would populate *Varekai*'s forest, Champagne and company turned to Cirque's own history as traveling entertainers for inspiration. In their view, Cirque and its audience are a community ever changing and on the move, where strangers become friends and family.

"I wanted to confront the main character with strangers. We constantly meet strangers, and we experience fascination and fear. We're curious about them, but also a little hostile toward them," explains Champagne. "So I created a large family of characters who have lived this experience, a kind of millennial family of nomads who survive in this enchanted forest."

For Champagne, it is essential that the audience, too, feel part of the forest community. "When the audience enters the show, we want them to feel they've entered a kind of enchanted forest," he says. "Because, in a way, the audience is part of that family, too. When two thousand people go 'Ah!' at the same time, it creates fellow feeling."

The vagabond theme in *Varekai* can be heard in its score. "In *Varekai*, you're looking at this tribe, maybe at another level of consciousness, a kind of gypsy camp," explains composer Violaine Corradi. "We wanted to merge urban beats into the gypsy thing. There's a lot of violin in the show, regular violin and electric violin. Even when you think you're hearing an electric guitar, it's a violin."

AN EVER-EVOLVING SHOW

Like all Cirque shows, *Varekai* is constantly changing. *Varekai* grows while its acrobats find their place as performers within its particular emotional and psychological context.

"*Varekai* has evolved enormously since its premiere in 2002. The whole show became more concrete. It found a better expression of itself," says Nicolette Naum, the show's artistic director. "There are a lot of acts that have gone through an impressive evolution, both artistically and acrobatically. The acrobats have evolved as artists. They've been able to grow out of the constraints of technique, and to evoke emotions."

Over time, according to Nicolette Naum, "*Varekai* is finding itself. There's a power emerging from it. Eventually, it will find a form where we say, 'Ah! That's it!'"

TAKING FLIGHT

Varekai's message is that there is comfort after chaos. "With *Varekai*," says Dominic Champagne, "I wanted to say that, if things sometimes seem difficult to us, we have to live that difficult experience all the way through to get to the light on the other side."

For Guy Laliberté, *Varekai* was proof that, even through constant change, Cirque du Soleil would find its way. "*Varekai* gave me hope that Cirque du Soleil will last. It allowed us to confirm that Cirque's power isn't just in individuals, it's in our ability to attract talent. That ability is more important than any individual, myself included. That's extremely important in the writing of Cirque du Soleil's next chapter. I'll help write it, but whatever happens after that will be up to others."

16/

17/

18/

15/
STELLA UMEH, SUSANNA DEFRAIA
SCALAS, HELEN BALL, CINTHIA BERANEK,
ZOE VICTORIA TEDSTILL, RAQUEL KARRO
IN THE TRIPLE TRAPEZE ACT.

16/
ANTON CHELNOKOV, ICARUS IN THE
FLIGHT OF ICARUS ACT.

17/
THE THRILLING CLOSING ACT,
RUSSIAN SWINGS.

18/
LEFT TO RIGHT: VALENTIN MENJEGA,
ROMECH MOURTAZOV, MAXIM
LEVANTSEVICH, ALEXEI ANIKINE, SERGIY
BOBROVNYK AND EVGUENI TARAKANOV.

THE CREATORS

AS CIRQUE DU SOLEIL EVOLVES, IT RELIES ON AN INCREASING NUMBER OF CREATIVE PERSONS TO PRODUCE ITS SHOWS. "MY DREAM HAS ALWAYS BEEN TO ATTRACT THE BEST TALENT THE WORLD HAS TO OFFER TO CIRQUE, AND THAT DREAM IS STILL ALIVE. I HOPE THAT THE STUDIO CONTINUES TO BECOME A HOME TO CREATIVE PEOPLE ALL OVER THE WORLD." WHILE THIS BOOK HIGHLIGHTS THE WORK OF SOME OF THEM, THERE ARE MANY MORE WHO HAVE BEEN PART OF THE CIRQUE STORY. "EACH OF THEM," EXPLAINS LALIBERTÉ, "IS ESSENTIAL TO WHAT WE DO. THEY DESERVE ALL THE CREDIT IN THE WORLD."

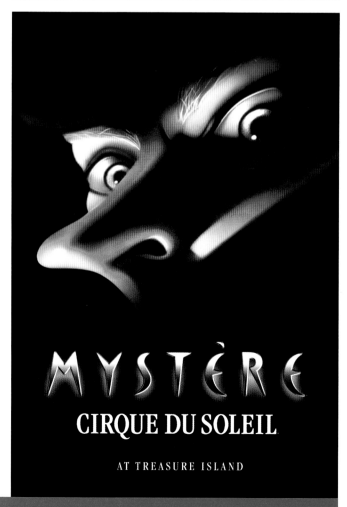

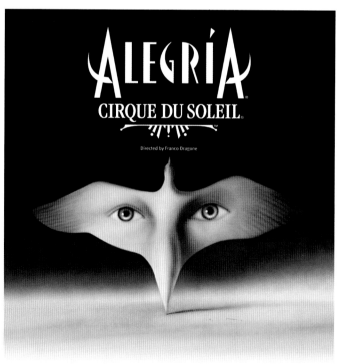

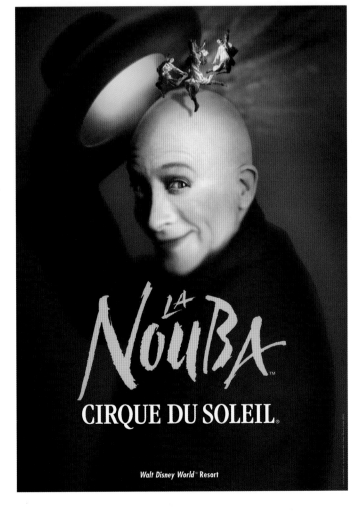

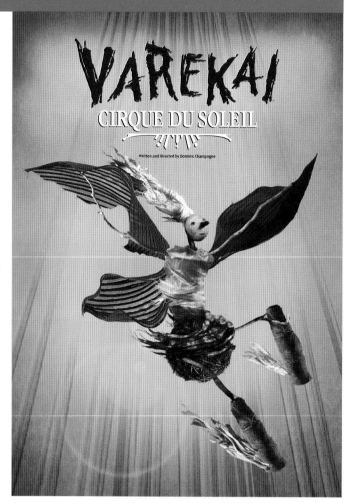

Since 1984, Cirque du Soleil's creators have included Catherine Archambault, François Barbeau, Michel Barette, Rudy Barichello, Angelo Barsetti, René Bazinet, Jacky Beffroi, Jean Bégin, François Bergeron, Lin Yung Biau, Normand Blais, Allison Brierly, Debra Brown, Pavel Brun, Jean-Yves Cadieux, André Caron, Guy Caron, Simon Carpentier, Sergeï Chachelev, Dominic Champagne, Stéphan Choinière, Warren Conley, Violaine Corradi, Didier Cousin, Michel Crête, Michael Curry, René Richard Cyr, Michel Dallaire, Jonathan Deans, Michel Deschamps, Pierre Desjardins, Manon Desmarais, Guy Desrochers, Marguerite Derricks, Nino D'Introna, Franco Dragone, Hélène Dubé, Pierre Dubé, René Dupéré, François Dupuis, Martin Ferguson, Mark Fisher, Holger Förterer, Sylvie Fréchette, Nathalie Gagné, Nol van Genuchten, Mark Giannetti, John Gilkey, Jacques Heim, André Hénault, Hélène Hétier, Wayne Hronek, Eiko Ishioka, Sara Joel, Benoit Jutras, Valeri Keft, Patrick King, Julie Lachance, Luc Lafortune, Guy Laliberté, Lucie Langlois, Francis Laporte, Catherine Lauda, Yves LeBlanc, Jean Leduc, Leonid Leikine, Hélène Lemay, Dominique Lemieux, Robert Lepage, Andrei Lev, Luis Lopez, Les Macloma, Mikhail Matorin, Michael McKenzie, Michael Montanaro, Cahal McCrystal, Natacha Merritt, Alexandre Moiseev, Richard Morin, Thierry Mugler, Gonzalo Muñoz Ferrer, Jaque Paquin, Slava Polunin, Stéphane Roy, Patricia Ruel, Basil Schoultz, Bill Shannon, David Shiner, André Simard, Alexandre Simonov, André Souci, Guy St-Amour, Gilles Ste-Croix, Hélène Tremblay, Marie-Chantal Vaillancourt, Andrew Watson, and Li Xining.

21/

CHAPTER
16

BEYOND THE STAGE

CDS IMAGES

➤ THE MAKING OF **VAREKAI** WAS CAPTURED IN THE EMMY AWARD-WINNING TELEVISION MINISERIES **FIRE WITHIN**, FIRST BROADCAST AT THE BEGINNING OF 2003. **FIRE WITHIN** WAS COPRODUCED BY GALAFIM OF MONTREAL AND CDS IMAGES, CIRQUE'S RAPIDLY EXPANDING MULTIMEDIA UNIT.

Over the past twenty years, more than two million soundtrack CDs from various Cirque shows have sold worldwide. Recordings of its touring shows for television, DVD, and video have encountered similar commercial and critical success. Cirque du Soleil has also released a theatrical feature (*Alegria*), an IMAX film (*Journey of Man*), and a number of documentaries.

Until recently, almost all of these multimedia experiences have been tied to a specific touring or resident show. In the future, Guy Laliberté hopes that CDS Images' output will not be fettered to the shows in the same way. "We're opening doors to new areas of artistic expression, giving people the means to express themselves from their own platforms, with their own passions."

The first step in this new direction is a variety television series that premiered in Canada on November 30, 2003: *Solstrom*.

02/

SOLSTROM: A CREATIVE LABORATORY

"In the past, Cirque used to film live shows and sell it to broadcasters," Daniel Lamarre says. "Now there's a challenge from Guy to develop our own television product. Don't start from live shows, start from TV. So we put together a creative team, and *Solstrom* was our laboratory. We're going through the same process for music and TV as Cirque did twenty years ago for its live shows."

Shot on a soundstage in Montreal, *Solstrom* is a dreamlike take on what happens to people when certain Cirque du Soleil characters come into their lives. Pierre Parisien, artistic director of the touring productions of *Alegría* and *Quidam*, was asked to act in the same capacity on *Solstrom*. "I had a word in trying to fit in acts from our shows into the TV shoot," he says. For Parisien, the work was "easy because our artists know their acts so well."

Jesko Von Den Steinen, who plays Eddie in *Saltimbanco*, nevertheless calls making his character live onscreen a "challenge." "Being on TV allows me to mime my character more, and try it in different contexts," he says. "It's a challenge to move from a medium of being live onstage in front of 2,500 people, and getting an immediate response and being truthful each time, and then going into a medium where it's not about being truthful, it's about hitting the right marks, it's about giving the impression of being truthful."

"Will Cirque be able to function in this structure?" asks Von Den Steinen. "Who knows?" For Laliberté, the jury is still out. "The live shows are where we come from," he comments. "It's our core business. I'm not sure where the balance will be with work in other media. At any rate, it will have to be measured by quality, not quantity."

03/

05/

"WE'RE OPENING DOORS TO NEW AREAS OF ARTISTIC EXPRESSION, GIVING PEOPLE THE MEANS TO EXPRESS THEMSELVES FROM THEIR OWN PLATFORMS, WITH THEIR OWN **PASSIONS.**"

01/
Maria Silaeva performs "Manipulation" in *Alegría*.

02/
Victor Bryndine, Alexei Liubezny, Alexey Poletaev, Ivan Saveliev, Anatoli Baravikou, Marcos Casuo, Tamir Erdenesaikhan, Victor Moiseev, Oleg Plotnikov, Viatcheslav Volkov and Myro Khetaguri in Russian Bar Act for *Solstrom*'s "Wind of Imagination" episode.

03/
Brad Denys appears as The Guide from *Varekai* in "Wind of Imagination."

04/
Henriette Gbou as Gaya from *Dralion* in "Once upon a Wind."

05/
Jordan and Nasko Balaktchiev (father and son) perform Hand-to-Hand as invited guests in "Once upon a Wind."

06/
Jeremy Brock, Paul Cameron, Marek Haczkiewicz, Vladislav Lissenkov, Artur Milon, Dan Niehauss, Zdzislaw Pelka, Grigoriy Shevchenko, and Rustam Vagidov perform Korean Plank in "Wind of Freedom."

07/
Gareth Hopkins, The Lizard in "Gone with the Winds."

07/

ZUMANITY

CHAPTER
17

REAWAKENING DESIRE

> **PULL BACK THE VEIL
> AND ENTER THE HUMAN ZOO,
> WHERE DESIRE SPARKS TO NEW LIFE
> AND INTIMACY AWAITS,
> WHERE THE SENSES ARE REAWAKENED
> AND DIVERSITY IS THE ONLY RULE.**

In September 2003, Cirque unveiled *"Another Side of Cirque du Soleil": ZUMANITY*, at the New York-New York Hotel & Casino in Las Vegas. In a radical departure from the world of the circus arts, *ZUMANITY* reinvents the erotic cabaret for mature audiences. Sensually combining song, dance, burlesque, and acrobatics, *ZUMANITY* challenges the spectator to reconsider his or her own outlook on human sexuality.

For Cirque, the show represented a new high-stakes gamble. How would Cirque's move into the relatively uncharted waters of adult entertainment be perceived? Could a live show by Cirque outside the circus realm work?

The road to *ZUMANITY* was long and tortuous, with plenty of naysayers along the way. Cirque weathered the storm by keeping its head down, and concentrating on creative integrity —in other words, business as usual.

01/
MARCELA DE LA VEGA LUNA, LA MUERTE.

02/
WASSA COULIBALY, THE AFRICAN QUEEN.

03/
PATRICK KING AS ATHON EXTRAVAGANZA.

ANOTHER SIDE OF CIRQUE DU SOLEIL

For Guy Laliberté, there were too many good reasons to deviate from the norm and do *ZUMANITY*.

The first reason is perhaps surprisingly practical. "We were offered the opportunity to do two more shows in Las Vegas," explains Laliberté, "which forced us to think about how we could make our products stand out from one another, so they don't cannibalize each other."

Another reason came from MGM MIRAGE, the project's backers. "Our partners at New York-New York wanted to make their casino more trendy, more 'Generation X,' more underground. The 'adult' part of that interested us."

Laliberté offers another, more personal reason for making *ZUMANITY*. "I thought the subject matter reflected who we are," he says. "We're a generation that has lived through more permissive times, so our approach to sexuality and eroticism is different. We were excited about the possibility of working with sexuality."

04/

Lastly, *ZUMANITY* offered a chance to work with riskier subject matter. "We wanted something edgier," says Laliberté. "Our previous shows have all been family-oriented and 'politically correct,' which is great. But we're human beings, we won't hide it. We're a bunch of happy campers. We like to live new experiences. *ZUMANITY* deals with some of those experiences."

For Daniel Lamarre, the decision to do *ZUMANITY* made perfect sense for a company that wants to remain at the forefront of creativity. "One of our biggest mistakes would be to think that we're invulnerable, and the temptation is always there," opines Lamarre. "Guy is so good at pushing boundaries, and taking risks.

He could have stopped at eight shows, but he said: 'No. I want to try a new show. I want to try a new category of show.' People say, 'Why are they doing that?' And we say: 'Because it's fun, and a little dangerous, and that's part of who we are.'"

When asked about the risk that *ZUMANITY* might not succeed, Lamarre answers: "Can we fail? Maybe. But we like to take risks, because they're creative risks. Without taking risks, people will look at us in five years and say, 'Oh, they're just a product of the nineties.' We don't want to be a product of the nineties, we want to be today's product."

04/
JESUS VILLA, FAUNA.

05/
ONE OF THE BOTEROS SISTERS PLAYED BY
LUCIENNE AND LICEMAR MEDEIROS.

05/

PART 3 | CHAPTER 17

ZUMANITY: REAWAKENING DESIRE

06/
THE NARCISSISTIC LAURENCE JARDIN AS MADEMOISELLE LOUP PERFORMS CONTORTION IN STRAPS.

07/
JOEY ARIAS IS MITZI LA GAINE, THE MISTRESS OF SEDUCTION, *ZUMANITY*'S RESIDENT DIVA AND GUIDE.

07/

SEX MAKES YOU HAPPY,

"WE WANT TO SHOW THAT SEX MAKES YOU HAPPY, BUT THAT IT CAN BE A LITTLE TROUBLING AT THE SAME TIME."

08/

08/
ZUMANITY EXPLORES A NEW FORM: A
FUSION OF DANCE, CABARET PERFORM-
ANCE, AND THE CIRCUS ARTS. THE JAIL
ACT IS PERFORMED BY CINTHIA AKANGA-
GUIBARD, ALEX CASTRO, JESSE ROBB,
JÉRONIMO GARCIA-CABRAL MEDINA,
ANTONIO DRIJA, UGO MAZIN, AND JESUS
VILLA.

09/
ZORIGTKHUYAG BOLORMAA AND
GYULNARA KARAEVA
IN WATER CONTORTION.

10/
ALEX CASTRO DANCES, AS
"ROMANTIQUE" LOOKS ON.

11/
LAURENCE JARDIN,
CONTORTION IN STRAPS.

09/

10/

11/

12/
AS MARCELA DE LA VEGA LUNA STANDS
BY, PATRICK KING AS ATHON AND
JOHAN KING SILVERHULT AS ARNO
PERFORM 2MEN.

13/
SARA JOEL AND STEPHAN CHOINIÈRE
PERFORM BODY2BODY.

12/

CASTING LIGHT ON DESIRE

ZUMANITY was cowritten and codirected by René Richard Cyr and Dominic Champagne. Champagne, working with Cirque for the second time, had some experience with cabaret. In 1992, he had written and directed a project of his own called *Cabaret Neiges Noires*, inspired by the life of Martin Luther King. René Richard Cyr—a respected Quebec writer, director, and actor working with Cirque for the first time—is a close friend and long-time collaborator of Champagne's. Before embarking on *ZUMANITY*, Cyr and Champagne had worked together on a number of Quebec television and stage productions.

Addressing their directorial intention, Cyr says: "We really want to light up desire. In our society, sex is everywhere, and used for everything. We want to be truly provocative. By 'lighting up desire,'" we mean bringing sex and love back to their rightful place, a more noble place. We see sexuality as a mysterious area, but a joyful one at the same time. In this show, we're exploring the space between the two. We want to show that sex makes you happy, but that it can be a little troubling at the same time."

For Cyr, that "troubling" aspect of the show is key to understanding *ZUMANITY* as *"Another Side of Cirque du Soleil." "Another side of Cirque du Soleil"* means this show isn't just about dreams and wonder," underlines Cyr. "We're exploring something darker, more disturbing, edgier. There's something fundamentally hidden about sexuality. When you make love to someone, you don't know what's in his or her mind, and they don't know what's in yours. There's a part of yourself that's even hidden to you. So it's like the dark side of the moon: we don't see it, but we know it's there."

Laliberté hopes the subversive aspect of *ZUMANITY* will open minds, and hearts. "The idea behind *ZUMANITY*," he explains, "is we hope, when people leave the theater, that they'll want to experience love with their partner, or partners, or friends. We hope they'll be more open about some of the rules we've been given, rules that are often manipulated by social clichés."

14/

REINVENTING THE CABARET

Just as Cirque had done with the circus, it hoped to help revive the cabaret with *ZUMANITY*. "We saw a challenge there," explains Guy Laliberté. "We were interested in using the cabaret revue as a creative platform, because it's an artistic form with lots of potential."

Thierry Mugler, an internationally renowned French fashion designer, was asked to costume design the show. At first reluctant to throw his hat in with Cirque, he was eventually won over by the chance to work in a revived cabaret form. "I began to fall in love with the project when the casting started and I saw the artists rehearsing," admits Mugler. "Seeing these extraordinary people was very moving: dancers, strippers, acrobats, fire-eaters ... so many different, interesting disciplines."

The set itself is inspired by the last great periods of the cabaret, at the turns of the nineteenth and twentieth centuries.

"As a set designer, the first thing I have to do is create a context," explains designer Stéphane Roy of his third show with Cirque. "That means creating a language. In this case, it's cabaret, and I decided to make a place inspired by Art Nouveau. Because it's an organic language, the result is not 'Art Nouveau' per se. It's my version of Art Nouveau. The feeling you should have is that it's like a huge tree growing. Everything has a curve and a spine so that sometimes it looks like a snake and turns into a tree ... everything in the set has an organic and physical language. I sometimes say that Art Deco is very phallic. Art Nouveau is more feminine, fallopian. In fact, if you look at how the performance space itself is structured, you can see that it's designed in the shape of fallopian tubes."

CELEBRATING DIFFERENCE

At its spiritual and emotional core, *ZUMANITY* is a celebration of human difference. "We wanted to talk about love," says Laliberté. "We wanted to break the rules about beauty, to say that beauty doesn't just reside in stereotypes. Our notion of beauty is much broader than a woman with a certain body type. We're working with a little person, larger women, all kinds of people. It brings us back to the fundamental notion of Cirque du Soleil: respecting differences, accepting people, and celebrating the idea that everyone is allowed to dream. You don't have to be a 'Perfect 10' to have a love life, and a fantasy life."

In true Cirque tradition, *ZUMANITY* emphasizes what makes us human first. As Thierry Mugler puts it, "This is a very human show. It's about human emotions, about being moved. Humanity is diverse. Yet, despite that diversity, everyone is searching, searching for love, searching for the sublime, trying to praise the cosmos."

16/

MGM GRAND

In April 2004, after two years of preparation, the cast and crew of a new resident show left Montreal to begin rehearsals in Las Vegas. The show, directed by internationally renowned director, playwright, and actor Robert Lepage, will premiere at the MGM-Grand Hotel and Casino in fall 2004.

The new show promises to be different from anything Cirque du Soleil has done. "We decided to create a show based more on circus skills than circus acts," explains director of creation Guy Caron. "It's based on a story, like a play. It will be an epic without words." Director Robert Lepage describes the show as a "theatrical-cinematographic experience."

The epic in question concerns a set of twins from a mythical time and place who become separated as adolescents during a struggle between two cultures. The story follows their adventures through different worlds and experiences as they attempt to reunite.

The show will be presented in a specially constructed theater that will be a technical achievement surpassing anything Cirque du Soleil has done to date. The theater and the show's set have been designed by Mark Fisher—the man behind the mammoth sets used by the Rolling Stones on their enormously successful tours in the 1990s. Many elements of the set, sound system, projections, and special effects will be made possible by products developed specifically for the show.

Continuing in the Cirque du Soleil tradition, the show promises to be a human experience above all. In the absence of words, the tremendous potential of the human body will be exploited to the fullest by the seventy-two-artist cast to convey the show's ambitious narrative and emotional arc.

CHAPTER
18

THE NEXT 20 YEARS

POSSIBLE FUTURES

**AFTER TWENTY YEARS,
CIRQUE DU SOLEIL HAS ENDED UP
WHERE IT STARTED:
FACING BOTH GREAT POSSIBILITIES
AND RISKS AHEAD.**

Each time it has negotiated a new turning point, Cirque du Soleil has demonstrated its ability to adapt and evolve. Whether it has been winning over new audiences, working with new partners, or venturing into new artistic territory, Cirque has responded by putting creativity first.

As Cirque du Soleil enters its third decade, its artists believe that the company's ability to attract and nurture creativity will be key to its future. "Cirque allowed us to do what we did," says Michel Crête. "In the future, Cirque can still be a facilitator to get other people together, who will do their own thing. It's the only way Cirque du Soleil will stay vital."

02/

"I believe very strongly in Cirque," adds Dominique Lemieux. "The human side of Cirque—the side that likes to tell stories and exceed itself, without being afraid of breaking its neck—will make Cirque last."

"Cirque should remain one of the important reminders of joy and beauty in the world," says Violaine Corradi. "There are always dreams that can come true, always worlds and realities beyond just the material world. As long as Cirque reminds people of this, Guy's name, 'Laliberté,' says it all: 'freedom.' He's a reminder of freedom, beauty, and madness."

As for Laliberté himself, he seems content to trust Cirque's future to the people he has gathered around him. "The soul of Cirque du Soleil is in each individual who works here and is doing his or her best to spread creativity with a positive attitude," he says. "The future of Cirque belongs to them."

"My commitment to Cirque is to keep supporting it creatively, as long as I sense a commitment to keep it going after I'm gone," he adds. "If we can preserve it, Cirque du Soleil has a future. If we're too greedy, if we forget to be humble, or become arrogant, then we put ourselves in danger."

After two decades at the helm, Laliberté is pleased with the journey, and ready to enjoy the fruits of a job well done. "Personally, what I want from Cirque now is to live a balanced life, to take care of my family, and enjoy what twenty years of work have brought me," he concludes. "I'm very happy with what I've done. I have the best job in the world. I've got angels and stars shining for me. It's an amazing life."

01/
TSEVEENDORJ NOMIN AND ULZIIBAYAR CHIMED PERFORM CONTORTION IN *ALEGRÍA*.

02/
HENRIETTE GBOU AS GAYA, FROM *DRALION*, LEADS A PROCESSION OF CIRQUE CHARACTERS AT THE MONTREAL STUDIO.
FROM LEFT TO RIGHT: ÂME FORCE (*DRALION*'S SINGER), THE BARON FROM *SALTIMBANCO*, AVIATOR FROM *QUIDAM*, LIZARD FROM *VAREKAI*, THE NUTS FROM *LA NOUBA*, MEMPHISTO FROM *MYSTÈRE*, *QUIDAM* FROM *QUIDAM*.

03/
THE NUTS (PAWEL AND WITEK BIEGAJ) BID ADIEU.

"THE HUMAN SIDE OF CIRQUE—THE SIDE THAT LIKES TO TELL STORIES AND EXCEED ITSELF, WITHOUT BEING AFRAID OF BREAKING ITS NECK—WILL MAKE CIRQUE LAST."

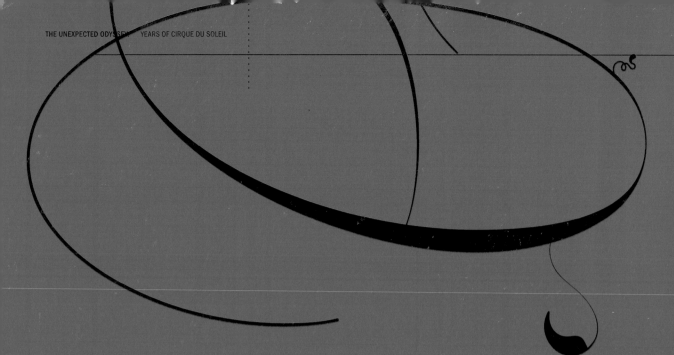

ACKNOWLEDGMENTS

Tony and Kris would like to thank everyone at Cirque du Soleil who was so instrumental in helping us put this book together. These include Rodney Landi, Geneviève Bastien, Marie-Josée Lamy, Brigitte Mezzetta, Kerry Knapp, Éric Chenoix, France Guillemette, Agathe Valissant, Carmen Ruest, Josée Bélanger, Louise Simoneau, Hélène Dufresne, Christiane Barette, Nedjma Belbahri, Émmanuelle Tétreault, Carole Trudel, Serge Côté, Nicole Ollivier, Benoît Quessy, Louise Plamondon, Annabelle Leblond, Francine Desrosiers, Lucien Bernèche and the indefatigable Louise Paquet. They extend a special thanks to Renée-Claude Ménard, without whose tireless efforts and constant vigilance this book would not have seen the light. They would also like to thank the people who welcomed them so warmly on their tour of Cirque shows, including Marianne Dodelet, Matthew Jessner, Magdelena Vandenberg, Joe Walsh, Jean-Jacques Pillet, Jola Biejag and Brigitte Warner. They would also like to thank Diesel Marketing of Montreal, under whose auspices they first got to work with Cirque, for its support and encouragement.

Tony thanks Christopher Sweet of Harry N. Abrams for his editing assistance. He also thanks each of the warm and generous individuals interviewed for this book for their time and assistance. All of them were eager to provide their perspective on Cirque's first twenty years, and Tony is sorry there wasn't space to include everything they said. These include Guy Laliberté, Gilles Ste-Croix, Guy Caron, René Dupéré, Serge Roy, Franco Dragone, Michel Crête, Dominique Lemieux, Lyn Heward, Daniel Lamarre, Michael Rosenberger, Carolyne Vita, Andriy and Maxsim Vintilov, Doxana and Daria Vintilova, Nicolle Liquorish, Yvon Cloutier, Gilles St-Amant, Marc Sohier, Linda Bélanger, Isabelle Dansereau Corradi, Oleg Ouchakov, Tatiana Gousarova, Johanne Gélinas, Nicolette Naum, Violaine Corradi, Vincent Gagné, Sylvie Galarneau, Jesko Von Den Steinen, Paul Bowler, Magalie Drolet, Simon Tinhan, Micheline Doucette, Natasha Hallett, Danielle Rodenkirchhcen, François Dupuis, Brian Dewhurst, Nicholas Dewhurst, Cécile Ardail, Anja Wyttenbach, Nathalie Bollinger, Terry Bartlett, Pierre Parisien, Konssntantin Besstchetnyi, Witek Biegaj, Natalia Pestova, and Yves Descoste.

Tony also thanks his wife, Julie, and children, Sophie and Max, for their support during this project. He dedicates this book to the loving memory of his grandfather, Andrej Ruszkowski, for pointing the way.

Kris thanks Nicolas St-Cyr for helping him design and art direct this book, Christian Bélanger for contributing his type-setting skills, Kevin Masse for just-in-time design help, and Norman Terrault for his contribution to overall structure. He thanks Raphael Daudelin, Pierre Desmarais, and Joanne Fillion for their constructive criticism. He also thanks J. F. Bouchard, Philippe Meunier, and Bertrand Cesvet of Diesel for encouraging him to work outside the box. He dedicates this book, with love, to his better half, Nadine Boileau, and their son Lucas, who was born during its design.

PHOTO CREDITS

COVER:

SKY: ROBERT GLUSIC/GETTY IMAGES
BEACH: SÉBASTIEN COIN

INTRODUCTION: VÉRONIQUE VIAL

PART 1:
FRONTISPIECE: FRANÇOIS RIVARD

CHAPTER 1:
FIG. 1:   GUY LALIBERTÉ
FIG. 2:   PRIVATE COLLECTION, GILLES STE-CROIX

FIGS. 3, 4, 5:   JEAN ST-CYR
FIG. 6:   CLAUDEL HUOT
FIG. 7:   FRANCOIS RIVARD
FIG. 8, 9:   PRIVATE COLLECTION, GUY LALIBERTÉ

CHAPTER 2:
FIGS. 1, 2, 4:   PRIVATE COLLECTION, GILLES STE-CROIX
FIGS. 3, 11, 22:   DANNY PELCHAT
FIG. 5, 9, 18:   PRIVATE COLLECTION, JOSÉE BÉLANGER
FIG. 6:   CIRQUE DU SOLEIL COLLECTION
FIG. 8:   RICHARD GEOFFRION
FIGS. 7, 12, 19:   PRIVATE COLLECTION, CARMEN RUEST
FIGS. 13, 14, 20:   FRANÇOIS RIVARD
FIG. 16:   CLAUDEL HUOT
FIG. 17:   PRIVATE COLLECTION, HÉLÈNE DUFRESNE

FIG. 21:   CIRQUE DU SOLEIL COLLECTION
FIGS. 23, 24:   C.I.O./COLLECTIONS DU MUSÉE OLYMPIQUE

CHAPTER 3:
FIG. 1, 5:   CIRQUE DU SOLEIL COLLECTION
FIG. 4:   GUY LALIBERTÉ
FIG. 6:   ARCHIVES NATIONALES DU QUÉBEC À
                        QUÉBEC, E10, D84-365, P2 / CIRQUE DU
                        SOLEIL—GASPÉ / DANIEL LESSARD,
                        JUNE 1984

CHAPTER 4:
FIGS. 1, 2:   COLL. TOHU, CITÉ DES ARTS DU CIRQUE—
                        FONDS JACOB—WILLIAM, MONTRÉAL
FIG. 4:   DANNY PELCHAT
FIG. 5:   RICHARD MAX TREMBLAY
FIG. 7:   KRIS MANCHESTER
FIG. 8:   JEAN-FRANCOIS LEBLANC
FIG. 9:   DANNY PELCHAT

CHAPTER 5:
FIG. 1:   ROBERT FRÉCHETTE
FIG. 2, 3:   DANNY PELCHAT

CHAPTER 6:
FIG 1:   GUY LALIBERTÉ
FIG 2:   JEAN-FRANÇOIS LEBLANC
FIG 5, 11:   CIRQUE DU SOLEIL COLLECTION
FIG 7:   AL SEIB

351

FIG 9: VÉRONIQUE VIAL
FIG. 10: DANY PELCHAT

PART 2:

FRONTISPICE: ÉRIC PICHÉ

CHAPTER 7:

ALL PHOTOS: JEAN-FRANÇOIS LEBLANC

CHAPTER 8:

ALL PHOTOS AL SEIB, EXCEPT:
FIG. 3: KRISTIAN MANCHESTER
FIGS. 9, 10: NICOLAS RUEL
FIGS. 12, 13: CIRQUE DU SOLEIL COLLECTION

CHAPTER 9:

ALL PHOTOS AL SEIB, EXCEPT
FIG. 2: KRISTIAN MANCHESTER
FIG. 5: JOHN GURZINSKI

CHAPTER 10:

ALL PHOTOS AL SEIB
FOOTNOTE:
FIG. 11: ERIC ST-PIERRE
FIGS. 12–16: LYNE CHARLEBOIS

CHAPTER 11:

ALL PHOTOS AL SEIB, EXCEPT:
FIG 7: JAN SWINKELS
FIG. 13 MATHEUZ MANIKOWSKI
FIGS.14, 17: KRISTIAN MANCHESTER
FIG. 16: KRISTIAN MANCHESTER
AND NICOLAS RUEL

CHAPTER 12:

ALL PHOTOS VÉRONIQUE VIAL, EXCEPT:
FIGS. 21–23, 25–28: MATHEUZ MANIKOWSKI
FIG. 24: AL SEIB

CHAPTER 13:

ALL PHOTOS VÉRONIQUE VIAL, EXCEPT:
FIG 4, 11, 12: MATHEUZ MANIKOWSKI
FIG.16: ALEX LEGAULT
FIG. 17: ERIC PICHÉ
FIG. 18: JULIE D'AMOUR-LÉGER
FIG. 19: PIERRE MANNING
FIG. 20, 22 MATHEUZ MANIKOWSKI
FIGS. 21, 23: KRISTIAN MANCHESTER

CHAPTER 14:

ALL PHOTOS AL SEIB, EXCEPT:
FIGS. 14, 16, 17, 18: VÉRONIQUE VIAL
FIG. 15: MATHEUZ MANIKOWSKI

PART 3:

FRONTISPICE: AL SEIB
P. 288: COLLECTION CIRQUE DU SOLEIL
P. 289: NICOLAS RUEL

CHAPTER 15:

ALL PHOTOS VÉRONIQUE VIAL, EXCEPT:
FIGS. 2, 4, 6, 8, 10, 11: JEAN-FRANÇOIS GRATTON

CHAPTER 16:

ALL PHOTOS MATHEUZ MANIKOWSKI, EXCEPT:
FIG.1: AL SEIB

CHAPTER 17:

ALL PHOTOS JERRY METELLUS

CHAPTER 18:

01/AL SEIB
02/03 MATHEUZ MANIKOWSKI